CFA Institute

AF885283

RESTRICTING SALES INDUCEMENTS

Perspectives on the Availability and Quality of Financial Advice for Individual Investors

CFA Institute is the global association of investment professionals that sets the standards for professional excellence. We are a champion for ethical behavior in investment markets and a respected source of knowledge in the global financial community.

Our mission is to lead the investment profession globally by promoting the highest standards of ethics, education, and professional excellence for the ultimate benefit of society.

ISBN: 978-0-938367-83-3
December 2013

Contents

CE Qualified Activity CFA Institute This publication qualifies for 2 CE credits, inclusive of 2 SER credits, under the guidelines of the CFA Institute Continuing Education Program.

Executive Summary

Access to high-quality financial advice for investors is undoubtedly a priority of financial regulators around the world as well as investors. But oftentimes, retail investors fail to see value in the financial advice available to them for a number of reasons. The reasons range from behavioural biases or a lack of transparency in fees to the erosion of trust because of headlines reporting mis-selling scandals in their markets.

Mis-selling, from the Lehman mini-bonds scandals in Hong Kong and Singapore at the height of the financial crisis,[1] to the selling of payment protection insurance (PPI) in the United Kingdom,[2] to the selling of hybrid products to retail investors in Spain,[3] has often been driven by sales and distribution structures with inherent conflicts of interest. Such structures can incentivise advisers and other financial professionals to put their own interests above the needs of their clients. In addition, many investors simply do not understand the complex series of costs and fees included in the financial products they purchase—costs that are not always disclosed in the most transparent manner.

In recent years, a number of markets, including Australia, Canada, India, the Netherlands, Switzerland, the United Kingdom, and the United States, have launched initiatives to improve access to financial advice, by both bringing greater transparency to the financial advice industry as well as addressing the problem of mis-selling. These initiatives have included improvements in the clarity required of financial advisers in reporting fees and conflicts of interest, or in some cases, limits or bans on **inducements** (payments, commissions, gifts, or kickbacks associated with the sale of investment products, often paid to advisers by distributors). Other markets are still in the evidence-gathering and decision-making stage, contemplating how best to increase the quality, availability, and independence of investment advice locally and reduce the risk of mis-selling, while pondering the trade-offs of the different options for reform. The structure of inducement prohibitions and cost transparency initiatives for advisers varies from

[1]Tom Holland, "Five Years Later, What Has the Mini-Bond Scandal Taught Us?" *South China Morning Post* (18 September 2013): www.scmp.com/business/article/1311841/five-years-later-what-has-mini-bond-scandal-taught-us.

[2]Jennifer Thompson, "Guidance Given for New PPI Products," *Financial Times* (24 January 2013): www.ft.com/cms/s/0/36a25b86-6637-11e2-bb67-00144feab49a.html#axzz2g0iqwefS.

[3]Sonja Dowsett and Greg Mahlich, "Spanish Regulator Says to Act Against Mis-Selling of Bank Debt," *Reuters* (29 May 2013): http://uk.reuters.com/article/2013/05/29/uk-spain-banks-idUKBRE94S14H20130529.

market to market. Because of recent regulatory activity throughout the world, many investors are now or soon will be operating under a new financial adviser–client relationship, resulting in a significant shift in the treatment of financial adviser inducements.

Inducements: Payments, commissions, gifts, or kickbacks associated with the sale of investment products, often paid to advisers by distributors.

This report explores the efforts that regulators and policymakers around the world have undertaken to bring higher-quality financial advice to investors, as well as the solutions that a number of regulators have implemented or proposed to address the problem of mis-selling. Included in this review are the insights of CFA Institute members who were asked to share their thoughts about potential solutions to reduce the risk of mis-selling—from increased transparency to outright bans of inducements—as well as their views on the investment landscape that would result from the implementation of each choice.

Summary of Findings

- Larger financial institutions are moving away from providing advisory services to smaller clients because of a lack of economic incentive to serve those clients.

- In markets that ban commissions, new platforms with direct-to-consumer or low-cost/low-service investment options are expected to proliferate. This shift may result in aggressive direct-to-consumer advertising of financial products, a practice that may lead to instances of inappropriate investments sold to retail clients without proper oversight.

- A lack of proper enforcement of existing rules meant to combat mis-selling and inducement abuses is also a problem because a number of regulators lack either the resources or the ability to enforce investor protections already in existence.

- Retail investors tend to prefer a commission model to a fee-for-service model, which complicates the move toward fee models in markets that have banned commissions and may result in a large underserved population.

- Investors often fail to understand just how much they are paying advisers, whether they are operating under a commission or a flat-fee structure. Greater transparency requirements and more investor education will help investors make better-informed decisions.

- Most of the reforms around inducements have taken place in the past few years. Investor behaviour and response to new products and advice schemes are not entirely predictable, and reactions in markets where reforms have been introduced should be closely observed.

- CFA Institute members who responded to a CFA Institute survey stressed the importance of improving transparency and disclosure and were wary of any policy reform that would diminish the incentives to open distribution networks or reduce the accessibility of investment advice for small retail investors.

Summary of Problem and Policy Considerations

Advisers who provide advice to investors often serve in a conflicted capacity because in many cases, these advisers or the firms they work for are earning more from inducements than they are in management fees from their clients. In some markets, regulators have decided to eliminate these conflicts altogether by banning inducements. Such action could have substantial and long-lasting consequences, both positive and negative.

Bans on inducements and the rules that would accompany such legislative actions will eliminate some conflicts of interest from the market for financial services, may encourage improved training for advisers in some markets, and may produce simpler products for investors as well as require a higher duty of care from advisers in some jurisdictions. But there are concerns about some of the unintended consequences that a ban on inducements may bring, such as

- fewer firms targeting/servicing smaller investors,
- less product choice for investors,
- less competition among advisers as they exit a now less lucrative business,
- less access to advice for retail investors, and
- an increase in low-cost, information-only, execution-only business models.

A number of jurisdictions have chosen for now to forgo a ban on inducements to avoid some of these negative consequences, believing that a seismic shift in the financial advice industry is not in the best interests of practitioners or investors at this time. Regulators in such markets have largely decided that *increased transparency* can best address the conflicts in the adviser–investor relationship without the potential negative consequences of an outright ban on inducements.

Transparency should be part of any solution aimed at addressing mis-selling because *simplified disclosures* that give investors the information they need to make informed decisions can only improve the investment experience. *Transparency should start with fee transparency*, including a more informative breakdown of the fees that investors pay. *Investors need to be informed about all the fees that they are paying and about the origin of each of those fees* (from the adviser, the distributor, or any other participant). It is also important to pursue *uniformity in fee disclosures* across jurisdictions to allow comparability of fees across markets, especially in the EU, where cross-border financial transactions are more common.[4] But there is a limit to what increased transparency can achieve because investors are subject to behavioural biases and cognitive limitations.

Simplified Disclosure in the EU—It's Complicated

KIID and KID

The KIID (Key Investor Information Document)

The KIID is a follow-on of the simplified prospectus within UCITS (Undertakings for Collective Investment in Transferable Securities) legislation. It is a short one- to two-page pre-contractual information document for all UCITS. UCITS is being revised in the UCITS V package. The KIID will not change in UCITS V but will probably undergo a reform in UCITS VI. UCITS VI and the KIID might be taken up by the European Commission at the same time and will most likely be handled by the new Commission starting in 2015.

The following are the main disclosure requirements in the KIID:

1. Objectives and investment policy
2. Synthetic risk and reward profile
3. Charges
4. Past performance
5. Practical information

[4]European Commission, "Packaged Retail Investment Products" (2013): http://ec.europa.eu/internal_market/finservices-retail/investment_products/index_en.htm; Rhodri Preece, "Packaged Retail Investment Products: Investor Disclosure Considerations for a Key Information Document," *CFA Institute* (September 2013): www.cfapubs.org/toc/ccb/2013/2013/10.

UCITS V has gone through a partial vote in the European Parliament plenary but awaits a final vote. Current expectations are that a final vote will take place before April 2014. The importance of finalizing UCITS V for the KIID lies in the fact that the UCITS VI revision is already being discussed and a timetable needs to be created for the progressive replacement of the KIID by the KID.

The KID (Key Information Document) Package

The European Commission proposed the KID, previously known as the PRIPS package, for all investment products that are packaged (including insurance). In the current discussions in the ECON Committee in the European Parliament, there are members seeking to enlarge the scope to shares and bonds, as well as issues on liability for information provided. The KID is much broader in scope than the KIID, and the Commission plans to merge the KID and the KIID in the UCITS VI revision.

Investor education is needed so that investors can make informed decisions. All the information in the world is not useful if investors do not know what to do with it or how to interpret it. The need for investor education is heightened in jurisdictions that have banned inducements. Investors in those jurisdictions with fewer assets to invest may find themselves underserved by larger firms, necessitating a move to execution-only businesses that are low cost but offer little or no advice.

Investors' behavioural biases and habits need to be addressed through education as well. Numerous studies show that investors often hold ingrained misperceptions about the cost of financial advice. Often investors believe investment advice should be free and will resist paying a fee for advice, even a fee that is relatively nominal and not recurring.

Although low-cost investing with no advice attached may be right for the well-informed, financially literate investor, regulators and investment firms need to work together to promote *greater investor access to quality, unbiased investment advice* that falls along a continuum from those needing almost no advice to those needing a great deal. A financial market with only two real levels of advice—high touch and no touch—leaves those investors in the middle, which is most investors, without options. These market investors in the middle will not need the same level of advice as high-net-worth individuals with tax and estate planning concerns, but they will definitely need some advice around such issues as saving for retirement,[5] education, or

[5]In this report we are mainly focusing on investors investing for themselves in non-workplace-based schemes. The advice given to workplace-based pension plans is beyond the scope of this paper.

other expensive life events. The fear is that a ban on inducements may leave such individuals without the advice they need in such matters. The advice given also needs to be *high-quality advice* because better access to low-quality advice does not do investors much good.

Financial services providers can also differentiate their products to better serve investors with diverse needs; for example, offer more basic products to investors with more straightforward needs, such as saving for education or retirement, while offering more complex products—likely with higher fees—to those in need of more specialised advice.

Financial firms can promote a more investor-friendly model that eliminates a major conflict of interest for advisers by *revising commission and remuneration structures* to eliminate those that encourage volume sales (tiered commissions).

Setting equal commission levels (as a percentage of management fee) for all products in the same category could also help eliminate some conflicts of interest in the adviser–client relationship.

Consistent and quality adviser training is needed to promote high-quality advice as well as help eliminate conflicts when possible and mitigation when conflict elimination is impractical. Advisers need to be trained to put their clients' interests first and to always disclose potential conflicts to clients.

Finally, to foster greater competition in the marketplace, regulators should explore ways to promote distribution models with what is called an "*open-architecture*", which allows bank or insurance company clients to have a choice of financial products issued by other institutions, thereby increasing product competition in the marketplace.

Introduction

Mis-selling is not a new problem. It is an issue that CFA Institute members have been aware of for many years and one that continues to resonate in an industry in which trust in financial professionals globally is at historical lows.

As part of CFA Institute's 2014 Global Market Sentiment Survey, CFA Institute members were asked to rank six ethical issues facing their local markets from most serious to least serious. Mis-selling, broadly defined, was ranked as the most serious ethical issue globally.[6] In 2013, members in Europe, the Middle East, and Africa (EMEA) most frequently identified mis-selling of products by financial advisers as the top concern. Globally, members rated mis-selling as the second most pressing concern, second only to market fraud.[7] In 2012, mis-selling was ranked as the most serious ethical issue globally by CFA Institute members.

Because markets themselves differ in culture, customs, and existing rules governing the client–adviser relationship, a number of different approaches have been adopted to address mis-selling and grant investors better access to higher-quality financial advice. Australia and the United Kingdom have opted for some level of a ban on commissions in the client–adviser relationship (although there are some exceptions for which products are covered), whereas India has implemented a ban on commissions in the selling of mutual funds. Similarly, the Netherlands has already issued a partial ban in 2013 with a full ban on inducements going into effect in 2014. Within the European Union, investor protection remains largely the responsibility of its member states. In 2011, the European Commission proposed that a distinction be made between independent advice (no monetary inducements and a wide range of financial instruments) and other advice. The proposal was being discussed in the Parliament and the Council at the time of the drafting of this paper.

A number of regulators have decided to forgo banning commissions for now and have instead opted for increased transparency regarding adviser fees and commissions. Several of these markets have indeed discussed a ban on commissions but have chosen for now to focus on increased transparency first. They will perhaps hold a ban on commissions in reserve if increased transparency fails to bring investors better access to high-quality financial advice or adequately address the mis-selling issue.

[6]The survey was conducted September–October 2013. More than 5,900 CFA Institute members participated in the survey. Visit www.cfainstitute.org for the full results.
[7]2013 Global Market Sentiment Survey Results: www.cfainstitute.org/Survey/global_market_sentiment_survey_2013.pdf.

The purpose of this report is to explore the issue of inducements in the European Union as well as on a global level, discuss and evaluate the steps taken by policymakers and regulators around the globe, and assess the effectiveness of each approach. We will examine the status quo of certain markets by considering existing regulation, regulatory steps already taken, and the impact of regulation thus far.

To add to this market analysis, more than 26,000 CFA charterholders were surveyed regarding their thoughts on the various approaches to dealing with mis-selling. The results are discussed throughout this report and the full results of the survey can be found in the Appendix.

Global Market Expectations

Currently, no global consensus exists about whether increased transparency of commissions is sufficient to lead to better outcomes. But CFA Institute members seem to favour transparency over inducement bans (see **Table 1**).

Table 1. What are the most important reforms needed to combat mis-selling?

	Total	Americas	APAC	EMEA
Reforming pay structures at distributors, linking staff and senior management remuneration to good investment outcomes for clients	56%	54%	65%	54%
Completely banning commission payments by product producers	15%	15%	13%	15%
Reforming commission payment structures by product producers (to reduce incentives to favor unsuitable products), while retaining them at least partially	35%	34%	43%	31%
Requiring a minimum standard of professional qualifications	43%	41%	43%	48%
Requiring wider product offerings by all distributors	5%	5%	4%	7%
Improving disclosure of product information to clients	46%	44%	47%	48%
Mandating full disclosure of product cost structures to clients	65%	68%	55%	62%
Mandating clear disclosure of all commission payments received by distributors before investment	60%	64%	55%	51%
Improving redress possibilities for clients (in particular retail clients)	24%	27%	25%	14%
Improving enforcement by national regulators	23%	22%	27%	23%
Improving investor education	46%	44%	48%	51%
Other	6%	6%	5%	6%
No opinion	1%	1%	1%	2%
Unweighted Sample Size	514	158	91	265

In a survey conducted between 22 May and 28 May 2013, 65% of 514 CFA Institute members surveyed stated that full disclosure of product cost structures to clients was the most needed reform to combat mis-selling. This result was followed by 60% who thought that mandating clear disclosure of commission payments was an important reform (respondents could choose more than one answer). Only about 15% of respondents believed that a complete ban on commissions was necessary to combat mis-selling.

CFA Institute members might also advise regulators and lawmakers to pick different primary targets in combating mis-selling because internal remuneration structures at distributors and the selling culture of financial institutions were seen as larger causes for concern. As shown in **Table 2**, respondents cited inappropriate commissions (48%) as only the third most likely cause of mis-selling. That cause ranked behind inappropriate internal remuneration structures at distributors (70%) and selling pressure from other internal entities (63%).

Table 2. In your opinion, what are the main causes of mis-selling?

	Total	Americas	APAC	EMEA
Inappropriate commission payments by product producers	48%	48%	55%	41%
Inappropriate internal remuneration structures at distributors (skewed toward volume sales or specific products)	70%	68%	75%	71%
Selling pressure from other internal group entities	63%	63%	65%	60%
Lack of professional qualifications	32%	30%	31%	40%
Lack of transparency regarding product comparisons	36%	37%	31%	34%
Laziness	19%	23%	11%	14%
Other	6%	6%	8%	8%
No opinion	2%	3%	1%	1%
Unweighted Sample Size	514	158	91	265

Transparency alone, however, is not likely to be the only answer. Many retail investors currently lack sufficient financial education to understand the disclosures, and many of them do not bother to read disclosure documents in the first place.[8] What good is transparency if investors do not understand the information they are given?

[8]Robert A. Prentice, "Moral Equilibrium: Stock Brokers and the Limits of Disclosure," *Wisconsin Law Review*, vol. 2011, no. 6 (2011):1059–1107 (http://wisconsinlawreview.org/wp-content/files/1-Prentice.pdf).

Consequences of a Ban on Inducements

The argument about whether to ban inducements or increase transparency to combat mis-selling focuses on the ultimate consequences of such actions. CFA Institute members were asked, "If commission payments by product producers are banned completely, what consequences, if any, do you see occurring as a result?" The results are shown in **Table 3**.

Table 3. If commission payments by product producers are banned completely, what consequences, if any, do you see occurring as a result?

	Total	Americas	APAC	EMEA
Distributors will stop offering particular products altogether, so product choice will diminish.	30%	25%	42%	33%
Retail clients will refuse to pay fees for advice.	16%	10%	21%	32%
Small retail clients will not be able to afford advice.	29%	24%	43%	37%
Distributors will continue to offer advice, but will shrink the product offerings to those they continue to receive fees on.	46%	47%	42%	43%
Distributors will continue to offer advice, but will offer only "in-house" products (products from their own financial group).	38%	38%	32%	45%
Banks will stop offering advice altogether, and will steer client money into deposits.	12%	8%	23%	15%
Small distributors will go out of business, reducing distribution channel choice and reducing product and service choice.	25%	19%	35%	35%
Other	12%	13%	10%	11%
None—I don't see any consequences of a complete ban of commission payments by product producers.	12%	15%	5%	4%
No opinion	6%	6%	4%	7%
Unweighted Sample Size	513	157	91	265

The survey results indicate that CFA Institute members believe a ban on commissions will result in an investment landscape with less choice for investors and a market that underserves, or does not serve, smaller clients. Some of the ramifications of a ban on commissions are explored next.

Less Choice in Terms of Distribution Channels and Products

A ban on commissions may be an effective test of the role that commissions really do play in adviser recommendations. A significant portion of the CFA Institute membership thinks that if inducements are banned, distributors will reduce their product offerings to products for which they continue to receive fees (perhaps only selling internal products) or stop offering some products altogether—likely resulting in less choice for individual investors.

Incentives for Banks to Distribute Their Own Products

A ban on commissions for independent advisers could benefit banks, which could distribute their own products for funding reasons or because they are not covered by the ban. But a ban could also lower the incentive for financial institutions to offer more "independent" products. The result would be less competition among financial product providers and perhaps less than optimal choices for retail consumers.

Would the Small Retail Investor Be Properly Served or Left without Any Advice?

The requirement to disclose adviser charges puts a price tag on financial advice that has in many cases been unseen by retail clients. Under the commission model, there may have been the perception by some retail clients that financial advice was free only because the cost was hidden. Asking someone to pay what might be a few thousand pounds, euros, or dollars a year for an adviser is psychologically different than quoting a 0.5% or 1% ongoing charge—if that charge was even disclosed in the first place. People tend to be more averse to writing a check for a lump sum than to having expenses accrue and net against performance in a manner that they do not see.

A ban or partial ban on inducements may cause large financial institutions to see smaller retail customers as a low priority, and as a result they will likely move away from servicing smaller retail accounts. This shift has already happened in the United Kingdom.

Many financial institutions in the United Kingdom have cut back on offering mass-market retail advice. In June 2012, the Royal Bank of Scotland cited the new rules in cutting 618 adviser jobs.[9] In November 2012, Lloyds stopped face-to-face advice for anyone with less

[9]Gavin Finch, "RBS to Cut 618 Financial-Planning Jobs, Charge for Advice," *Bloomberg News* (19 June 2012): www.businessweek.com/news/2012-06-19/rbs-to-eliminate-618-financial-planning-jobs-charge-for-advice.

than £100,000 in assets after finding that most consumers were unwilling to pay a fee for the service.[10] HSBC cut up to 700 jobs, citing the Retail Distribution Rules (RDR) going into effect in January 2013 as the reason.[11]

In the United Kingdom, there is a concern that some salespeople will switch to pushing insurance products, which are not covered by the commission ban. There is also an expectation of consolidation among independent financial advisers (IFAs) in the United Kingdom as many respond to changes by leaving the business.

There is already a boom in smaller execution-only services in the United Kingdom (similar to the current landscape in the United States). These smaller firms see an opportunity that has offered a lucrative business model in other markets—it remains to be seen whether "do it yourself" retail clients will be best served by a low-cost/no-advice model. A related concern is where retail clients will find enough investment data or information to make informed investment decisions.

In Australia, the Future of Financial Advice reforms were implemented to improve the trust and confidence of Australian retail investors in the financial planning sector. The reforms include a ban on commissions in Australia, and the ban is expected to force Australian investors to adapt to a pure fee model—some blend of assets-under-management fees, retainer fees, or hourly fees. As in the United Kingdom, in Australia there are very few direct-to-consumer or low-cost/low-service investment options. These models are likely to gain ground in Australia in the coming years and offer low-advice/low-cost alternatives for investing. The question is whether these changes will result in aggressive advertising for direct-to-consumer financial products that leads to many instances of inappropriate investments being sold to retail clients.

Whatever the Reform, Increased Disclosure Is Part of It

No matter what one's position is on whether commissions should be banned, more transparency around commissions and fees can be expected in a number of markets around the world. Although Australia and the United Kingdom have chosen the route of commission

[10]Michelle Abrego, "Lloyds U-Turns and Scraps Plans for Mass Market Advice," *New Model Adviser* (27 September 2012): http://citywire.co.uk/new-model-adviser/lloyds-u-turns-and-scraps-plans-for-mass-market-advice/a621989.

[11]"HSBC to Cut 200 UK Jobs," *The Independent* (30 June 2011): www.independent.co.uk/news/business/news/hsbc-to-cut-700-uk-jobs-2304799.html.

bans, other markets, such as Canada, Hong Kong, India, Singapore, the United States, and the EU, have all decided to increase disclosures on the fees paid to financial advisers instead of outright commission bans.

Recent developments in Canada offer a practical example. Canadian regulators decided against a ban on inducements, instead opting for increased transparency. The 2012 Client Relationship Model (CRM) requires Canadian financial advisers to fully disclose to clients all transaction details, commissions, and fee breakdowns.

In the survey, CFA Institute asked its members how best to reform commission payments by product producers without a ban on commissions. Increased transparency—in the form of standards for cost disclosure—was overwhelmingly the most popular choice, as shown in **Table 4**.

Table 4. How, if at all, could commission payments by product producers be reformed without a complete ban?

	Total	Americas	APAC	EMEA
Revising commission structures to eliminate those that encourage volume sales (tiered commissions)	45%	41%	58%	46%
Providing only for minimum remuneration levels to compensate for distribution expenses incurred	17%	18%	15%	14%
Setting equal commission levels (as a fixed percentage of the management fee) for all products in the same category	32%	35%	24%	29%
Introducing clear standards for cost disclosures in the same way as there are standards for performance disclosure	68%	68%	62%	73%
Other	7%	8%	8%	4%
No opinion	5%	5%	5%	5%
Unweighted Sample Size	511	157	91	263

Whatever the Fee Structure, Investors May Be Unwilling to Pay

A 2012 survey by Rostrum Research[12] in the United Kingdom found that people were reluctant to pay a flat fee for financial advice. According to the survey, less than one in five (16%) of respondents said that they would be comfortable paying for financial advice from a retailer.

[12]Rostrum Research, "Retail versus Financial Services: The Battle for Consumer Trust," white paper (October 2012): www.rostrumresearch.com/downloads/rostrum-research-whitepaper-oct12.pdf.

They survey also found that 9 out of 10 consumers would only pay up to £25 for an hour of financial advice, well below the £50–£250 they would be expected to pay for such a service.

A report published by Deloitte[13] in 2012 predicted that a combination of investor apathy toward a pay-for-service model and a move by asset managers to service higher-net-worth customers would result in an underserved UK investor base:

> Combined, these changes mean that there will be up to 5.5 million disenfranchised customers who will either choose to cease using financial advisers or lack access to them. These customers, who account for 11 percent of UK adults, will represent a significant post-RDR advice gap (p. 2).

In a survey of 7,800 US households released in 2011 by Cerulli Associates,[14] about 47% of households surveyed preferred paying commissions whereas only about 27% preferred a fee based on amount of assets. About 18% of those surveyed said they preferred a negotiated fee and 8% preferred an hourly fee structure. About 33% of investors surveyed said they did not know how they pay for investment advice, and even more troubling, 31% said they thought such advice was free. Those who were unsure of how they pay for advice were most likely to be unhappy with their financial adviser, with 47% reporting dissatisfaction. About 27% of those who said they pay commissions reported being dissatisfied.

Investors were also unsure of the duty of care owed to them by their advisers. About 64% of those surveyed said they believe their financial adviser is held to a fiduciary standard of care, and 63% of clients of the largest broker/dealers said they thought that as well. In the United States, registered financial advisers are held to a fiduciary standard, but broker/dealers are held to a less stringent suitability standard.

Often investors say that they want a flat fee for advice—but then balk at the final cost of that advice. A 2013 survey by the Life Insurance and Market Research Association (LIMRA) found that 55% of Americans said they would prefer to pay a flat fee for financial

---

[13]Deloitte, "Bridging the Advice Gap: Delivering Investment Products in a Post-RDR World," Deloitte Insights Report (2012): www.deloitte.com/assets/Dcom-UnitedKingdom/Local%20Assets/Documents/Industries/Financial%20Services/uk-fs-bridging-the-advice-gap.pdf.

[14]Cerulli Associates, "The Evolving Retail Direct & Discount Brokerage Market: Distributing Through Third-Party Platforms (December 2011): https://external.cerulli.com/file.sv?F0000EM. Report is available for purchase.

advice, until they learned what such advice cost.[15] LIMRA found that only one in five consumers were willing to pay more than $100 for investment advice—an amount that likely would not get them much time with an adviser.

The average retail investor may be predisposed to be averse to upfront fees paid to advisers. A recent EU study explored investor decision making through the lens of behavioural economics, which attempts to look at how experiences and biases influence people's decision making.[16] The study found that

> A significant minority of people may be disproportionately averse to paying an up-front fee for advice. Between twenty and thirty percent of the online subjects displayed evidence of "narrow framing" and loss aversion, making them excessively averse to an up-front fee. There was no strong socio-demographic or attitudinal signature for this group of people (p. 10).

At the same time, the report suggests disclosure of conflicts of interest can lead to a loss of trust among consumers (i.e., knowing that there is a conflict reduces their willingness to rely on advice). So, either approach—commission ban or more transparency—is imperfect. The EU report does offer some suggestions on the transparency side; for example, a "health warning" may be necessary for people to understand the implications of a conflict of interest. The right sort of transparency can help, but context, location, and labeling are important from a behavioural perspective.

With regard to distribution, the report says that "Advice is ubiquitous in the retail investment market: about 80% of investments are made in a face-to-face setting, usually with an employee of the investment provider or a professional advisor. Furthermore, 60% of investors say their final choice of product was influenced by an advisor, while the advisor initiated the purchase on a quarter of occasions" (p. 385).

---

[15]Brian Anderson, "Middle-Income America Is Not Ready for Fee-Based Advice," LifeHealthPro.com (28 May 2013): www.lifehealthpro.com/2013/05/28/middle-income-america-isnt-ready-for-fee-based-adv.
[16]European Commission, "Consumer Decision-Making in Retail Investment Services: A Behavioural Economics Perspective" (November 2010): http://ec.europa.eu/consumers/strategy/docs/final_report_en.pdf.

EU Distribution Channels

Much has happened over the last decade to reshape the economic and investor landscape in Europe. The greater sophistication and more complex structure of financial markets, rapid technological developments, and the increase of third-party intermediated distribution models have enhanced the opportunities available to investors. In particular, the growth of open-architecture distribution models allows bank or insurance company clients a wider choice of financial products issued by other institutions. These models have helped promote greater competition in the marketplace.

The Legislative Procedure in Europe Explained

When the European Commission prepares a proposal for a legislative text, the European Parliament first assigns a committee responsible for drawing up its report on the proposal, with added committees giving their opinions. The committee, in this case the Economic and Monetary Affairs committee, appoints a member of the committee as Rapporteur to draft a report, which will be discussed and amended in the committee. Once the committee has voted on the report in a first reading procedure, a trilogue (or negotiation) will take place between the European Parliament and the European Council in order to reach a common position. The report is then voted on in the plenary of the European Parliament.

Because the UCITS legislation is a directive, the legislation is adopted by national legislators who have some freedom to determine the manner in which it is implemented. This freedom can lead to divergences and differences in market practice.

The KID package currently being discussed is a regulation, not a directive, which means that once the package is adopted by the European Parliament, the legislation will be transposed directly into national law with no divergences, creating a uniform platform across the EU.

At a simplified level, there are four main distribution channels in Europe: brokers or independent financial advisers, agents (tied or multi-agent), direct sales, and bancassurance.

Brokers or IFAs have no contractual agreements with any specific providers. Brokers offer advice on financial matters to their clients and recommend suitable financial products from a wider range of the market. In the United Kingdom, IFAs are responsible for about 70% of distribution, whereas in other markets, agents tied to banks or financial institutions are the primary method of distribution, as shown in **Figure 1**.

Figure 1. Fund Assets by Distribution Channel and Country

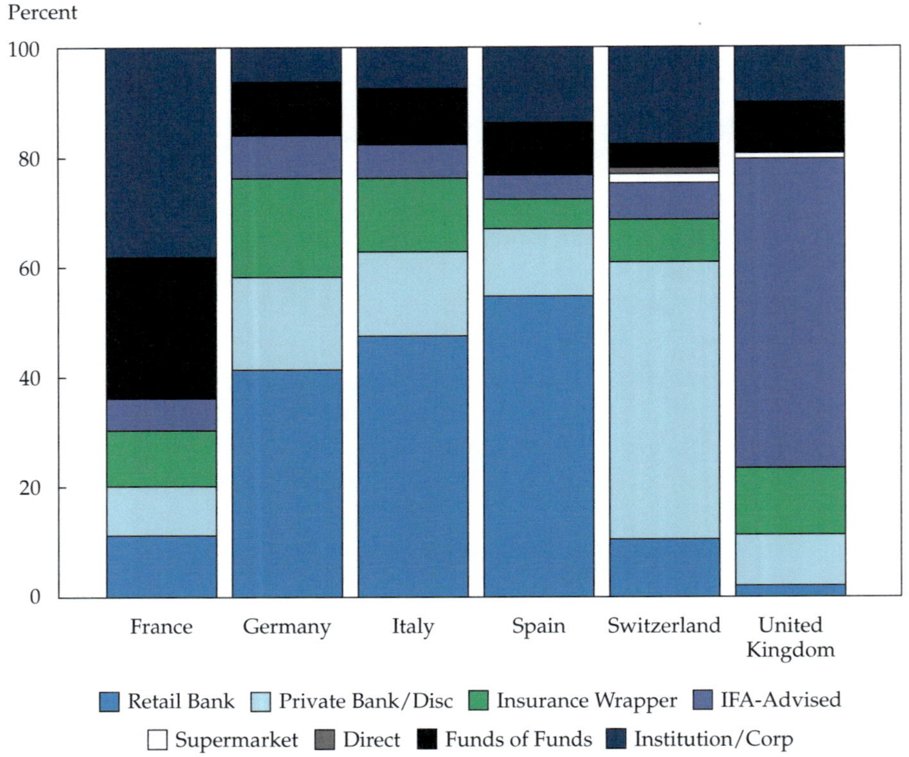

Sources: Based on data from Mackay Williams and Fund Radar.

Tied agents are intermediaries that only offer products from specific providers with which they have agreements. They can be either sole or multi-firm agents. Tied agents (generally tied to banks) represent, for instance, more than 50% of the distribution channels in Germany.

Bancassurance is an arrangement in which a bank and an insurance company form a partnership so that the insurance company can sell its products to the bank's client base. In European markets, banks and insurance companies that offer each other's products are often, but not always, part of the same corporate entity. Banks can earn additional revenue by selling the insurance products, while insurance companies are able to expand their customer base without having to expand their sales forces or pay commissions to insurance agents or brokers. Bancassurance arrangements are very common in Europe, where the practice has a long history. Today, the bancassurance channel accounts for more than 50% of the distribution in Austria, France, and Italy.

The sales forces of banks and insurance companies (including tied agent networks) are by far the dominant distribution model across Europe; in some countries, they account for more than 95% of the distribution of financial products.[17]

[17]Accenture, "How Bancassurance Can Dominate the UK Life Insurance Industry," Accenture Multi-Channel Distribution Consumer Survey (2010): www.accenture.com/us-en/blogs/accenture-blog-on-insurance/Media/Accenture_Bancassurance_PoV.PDF.

EU Regulation—MiFID I Legislation and Inducements

The original Markets in Financial Instruments Directive (MiFID I), adopted in 2004, was intended to harmonise regulation concerning investment services through the 30 member states of the European Economic Area (EEA). The main objectives of the law were to increase competition and consumer protection in investment services.

Almost 10 years later, there is concern among EU policymakers and supervisors that many firms complied with the letter of MiFID but not the spirit—that is, its high-level principles were not entirely implemented or enforced and clients' interests were often still not being put before those of advisers. A lack of appropriate follow-up concerning implementation and enforcement of MiFID I led to the creation of MiFID II, which is currently under negotiation. One of the main concerns with the effectiveness of MiFID I, which will still be an issue with MiFID II, is that it takes the form of an EU directive, and not an EU regulation, when it comes to addressing conflicts of interest in the distribution of financial products. An EU directive is not directly binding on member states, which are given flexibility in its implementation as national law. Inducement rules have been revised in discussions around MiFID II, indicating that the original provisions did not deal with inducements in a satisfactory manner.

The European Securities and Markets Authority (ESMA) and its predecessor, the Committee of European Securities Supervisors (CESR), drafted guidelines directed at national regulators and supervisors to bring consistency in MiFID I implementation, but with little result. Enforcement of inducement-related rules and other investor protection measures under MiFID I was low in most countries because different member states placed enforcement of the directive at different priority levels.

Some member states, notably the United Kingdom and the Netherlands, began reforms in their national markets in advance of the tabling of the MiFID II proposal. The most prominent reform dealt with the application of the RDR in the United Kingdom. The UK Financial Conduct Authority (FCA) will review the effectiveness and success of the RDR (in which they banned inducements) throughout 2014. The implementation of MiFID II proposals is not expected until 2014 or 2015 and allows regulators to impose more stringent requirements if they want—as the United Kingdom has done with RDR.

The current policy debate around the role and responsibility of distributors is multifaceted and complicated. Each EU member state has a different distribution structure and market culture. Disclosure and suitability requirements do exist under the current MiFID rules, although European investors continue to experience different levels of disclosure and services across products, distribution channels, and countries.

Limits to Disclosure

One of the remaining unsolved problems under MiFID I is that of disclosure. Article 26 of the implementing directive (2006/73/EC) stipulates that

> The existence, nature and amount of the fee, commission or benefit, or, where the amount cannot be ascertained, the method of calculating that amount, must be clearly disclosed to the client, in a manner that is comprehensive, accurate and understandable prior to the provision of the relevant ... service.

Article 26 also states that disclosure of inducements in "summary form" may be allowed by EU member states, as long as the investment firm provides further information at the request of the client. This rule has led to a lack of harmonisation in the implementation across the EU.

In the United Kingdom for example, the exact amount of commissions had to be disclosed before a transaction, whereas in other countries, financial advisers only needed to mention somewhere in the very long disclosures to investors that a financial firm may be receiving inducements, and—for funds, for example—that the firm would be receiving "between X% and Y% of the management fee" as commission. This band between X and Y could be quite wide, and because it was not mentioned in connection with a specific fund, it was impossible for retail clients to calculate the inducements for a given transaction.

Furthermore, commission disclosure is only one part of the costs an investor may incur. Even for such products as UCITS funds,[18] where a Key Investor Information Document (KIID) is mandatory, investors can only get information on the product-related costs, management fee, and so on, but not the costs related to acquiring the product. This lack of transparency is the result of the fragmentation of regulation in the EU and the different players in the supply chain of funds.

[18]Undertakings for Collective Investment in Transferable Securities (UCITS), Directive 2001/107/EC and 2001/108/EC, are a set of European Union Directives that aim to allow collective investment schemes to operate freely throughout the EU on the basis of a single authorisation from one member state.

The current MiFID II proposals have singled out commissions paid to independent financial advisers that operate in an open-architecture environment as being particularly detrimental to investors, and thus subject to a "partial ban". For some countries in Europe, MiFID II may open a window of opportunity for independent advisers to profile themselves firmly as independent. Advisers will have to decide whether they want to be called independent (which under MiFID II will require them not to accept inducements) or not to be called independent. If they were using the name "independent" before the reform, they will still have to choose.

The proposals also define independent advice as that given following an assessment of a sufficiently large number of financial products diversified by type, issue, or product provider. Therefore, providing advice on too narrow of a product type or offering is deemed not independent.

Because the proposed MiFID II does not ban inducements but only restricts the use of the term "independent advice" to distributors who do not accept inducements, it is uncertain how the market structure will develop. In the future, advisers will have to choose their business model. It will fall on supervisors to ensure that those advisers holding themselves out as independent offer broad market coverage and do not accept inducements. The details are to be determined in secondary legislation.

Remuneration structures at advisory firms and distributors can lead to conflicts of interest and mis-selling. But until 2012, there had been little focus on remuneration of staff, even though it plays a fundamental role in setting the incentives of sales staff.

Even strengthening rules for staff remuneration, however, is likely to leave untouched the issue of product choice, which can lead to suboptimal results for the clients. Until now, no efforts have been made in the EU to promote a more open architecture, which would allow clients to access most funds in the market, or at least those funds from fund families that are willing to allow their funds to be offered on such a platform.

Mandating open architecture could be equivalent to unbundling the distribution network of banks and insurers, perhaps obligating them not to deny access to their distribution platforms (upon a "fair" commercial compensation). The alternative is to introduce pre-contractual disclosure about the advice service itself (including disclosure on market coverage and the presence or level of inducements) and educate investors so that they are capable of understanding the wide differences existing between advice services. The proposal of the European Commission to reserve the label independent may be a step in this direction.

Currently, the cost of advice to retail investors is often paid by the product provider to the distributor in the form of a commission. This payment can be an upfront commission paid out of the initial subscription and/or an ongoing trail of commissions. Alternatively, the cost of advice can be met by fees paid directly by the end investor to the adviser. Under the commission-based model, it is not always easy for investors to determine the actual cost of advice; indeed, some mistakenly believe that this advice is provided for free. Existing MiFID rules require the disclosure of inducements, but disclosure is often provided as a formula (as commission is determined as a percentage of future net assets) rather than as an easy-to-understand fixed monetary amount. It is thus difficult for end investors to appreciate the value of the advice and to relate it to the cost of providing that advice. Unless end investors appreciate the value of advice, many perceive the fee-based advice as an additional cost and are, for the most part, unwilling to pay.

Fees from distributors can in some cases make up the bulk of the expenses paid by an investor when buying a financial product. A recent study broke down some of the expenses that European retail investors pay.[19] The report showed that in Europe, a retail equity fund shareholder pays about 175 bps in average total annual expenses reflected by a total expense ratio (TER); retail bond fund shareholders pays about 117 bps. Interestingly, the study showed that, on average, UCITS fund managers retain just 42% of TERs, whereas through retrocessions, distributors are paid 41% of the TER. About only 17% of TERs are used for operating expenses, such as custody, administration, transfer agency, and other costs.

Retrocession-based fees will most likely drop over time if they are made more transparent. Other fees may increase, but not always to the detriment of the investors. Higher professionalisation of advisers and thus higher-quality advice can lead to higher advice costs. But more professional advice can lead to better outcomes for investors. Would investors pay more for better-quality advice? It remains to be seen.

[19]European Fund and Asset Management Association, "Fund Fees in Europe: Analyzing Investment Management Fees, Distribution Fees, and Operating Expenses" (October 2011): www.efama.org/Publications/Statistics/Other%20Reports/EFAMA_Fund%20Fees%20in%20Europe%202011.pdf.

National Examples—Europe, Middle East, and Africa

In this section—and the two that follow—we will explore the approach to mis-selling and sentiment around the issue of inducement bans and increased transparency at the regional and individual market levels. This section explores the landscape in Europe, Middle East, and Africa (EMEA), and the other two sections explore attitudes and regulatory approaches in Asia Pacific (APAC) and the Americas.

As is shown in **Table 5**, there is much agreement between CFA Institute members in EMEA and the global membership concerning the most important reforms needed to combat mis-selling. Most CFA charterholders favor mandating full disclosure of product costs and mandating clear disclosure of all commissions to combat mis-selling; these two choices were the most picked solutions by survey respondents in EMEA and globally.

Table 5. What are the most important reforms needed to combat mis-selling?

	Total	EMEA
Reforming pay structures at distributors, linking staff and senior management remuneration to good investment outcomes for clients	56%	54%
Completely banning commission payments by product producers	15%	15%
Reforming commission payment structures by product producers (to reduce incentives to favor unsuitable products), while retaining them at least partially	35%	31%
Requiring a minimum standard of professional qualifications	43%	48%
Requiring wider product offerings by all distributors	5%	7%
Improving disclosure of product information to clients	46%	48%
Mandating full disclosure of product cost structures to clients	65%	62%
Mandating clear disclosure of all commission payments received by distributors before investment	60%	51%
Improving redress possibilities for clients (in particular retail clients)	24%	14%
Improving enforcement by national regulators	23%	23%
Improving investor education	46%	51%
Other	6%	6%
No Opinion	1%	2%
Unweighted Sample Size	514	265

Survey respondents in EMEA agree with those in the rest of the world in citing inappropriate remuneration structures as the main cause of mis-selling. Those in EMEA are more likely than their global counterparts to believe that a lack of professional qualifications leads to mis-selling, whereas they are slightly less likely to claim inappropriate commission payments as a main cause (see **Table 6**).

Table 6. In your opinion, what are the main causes of mis-selling?

	Total	EMEA
Inappropriate commission payments by product producers	48%	41%
Inappropriate internal remuneration structures at distributors (skewed toward volume sales or specific products)	70%	71%
Selling pressure from other internal group entities	63%	60%
Lack of professional qualifications	32%	40%
Lack of transparency regarding product comparisons	36%	34%
Laziness	19%	14%
Other	6%	8%
No opinion	2%	1%
Unweighted Sample Size	514	265

Table 7 deals with the EMEA perspective concerning the ramifications of an outright ban on commissions. Those in EMEA are more likely than global respondents to believe that small clients will not be able to afford advice if commissions are banned. Global survey respondents and those in EMEA are both concerned that distributors will reduce their product offerings.

Table 7. If commission payments by product producers are banned completely, what consequences, if any, do you see occurring as a result?

	Total	EMEA
Distributors will stop offering particular products altogether, so product choice will diminish.	30%	33%
Retail clients will refuse to pay fees for advice.	16%	32%
Small retail clients will not be able to afford advice.	29%	37%
Distributors will continue to offer advice, but will shrink the product offerings to those they continue to receive fees on.	46%	43%
Distributors will continue to offer advice, but will offer only "in-house" products (products from their own financial group).	38%	45%
Banks will stop offering advice altogether, and will steer client money into deposits.	12%	15%
Small distributors will go out of business, reducing distribution channel choice and reducing product and service choice.	25%	35%
Other	12%	11%

(continued)

Table 7. If commission payments by product producers are banned completely, what consequences, if any, do you see occurring as a result? (continued)

	Total	EMEA
None—I don't see any consequences of a complete ban of commission payments by product producers.	12%	4%
No opinion	6%	7%
Unweighted Sample Size	513	265

Table 8 explores survey respondents' thoughts concerning how commission payments could be reformed without resorting to a complete ban. All respondents across the globe and in EMEA believed that introducing clear standards for cost disclosure is the best reform available.

Table 8. How, if at all, could commission payments by product producers be reformed without a complete ban?

	Total	EMEA
Revising commission structures to eliminate those that encourage volume sales (tiered commissions)	45%	46%
Providing only for minimum remuneration levels to compensate for distribution expenses incurred	17%	14%
Setting equal commission levels (as a fixed percentage of the management fee) for all products in the same category	32%	29%
Introducing clear standards for cost disclosures in the same way as there are standards for performance disclosure	68%	73%
Other	7%	4%
No opinion	5%	5%
Unweighted Sample Size	511	263

There was little disagreement between global survey respondents and those in EMEA as to the seriousness of the potential loss of distribution channels and products that may occur with a ban on commissions (see **Table 9**).

Table 9. How serious do you consider the potential loss of distribution channels and/or the reduction of product range by distributors in case of restrictions or bans on commission payments?

	Total	EMEA
1 - Not serious at all	18%	12%
2	17%	18%
3	21%	18%
4	22%	28%

(continued)

Table 9. How serious do you consider the potential loss of distribution channels and/or the reduction of product range by distributors in case of restrictions or bans on commission payments (continued)

	Total	EMEA
5 - Very serious	16%	17%
No opinion	6%	7%
Unweighted Sample Size	513	265

United Kingdom

Regulator and Inducement Reforms

The Retail Distribution Review initiative was launched by the Financial Services Authority (FSA) in June 2006 to reorganise the fee structures between investment managers and their distributors as part of a strategy to ensure that adviser clients are treated fairly. The Financial Conduct Authority, one of the successors to the FSA, believes that by replacing commissions with upfront fees, any bias toward commission paying products is removed, which will, in turn, lead to quality advice and enhance the suitability of products for clients' return–risk profile. In the place of commissions, advisers can charge upfront agreed-on fees for ongoing investment advice, subject to disclosure indicating that their services are either "independent" or "restricted" to a particular product range. After several years of consultation, the rules were adopted and finally came into effect on 31 December 2012. The rules are aimed at

- improving the disclosure to clients for services provided by the firm (type of products and service offered, cost of advice, and how customers will pay for it),
- addressing the potential for adviser remuneration to bias recommendations, and
- raising professional standards for advisers and introducing new minimum standards of qualifications and professionalism.

The inducements ban will not cover everyone getting financial advice in the United Kingdom, and it will not cover all financial products. Only UK-based firms are subject to the RDR, so non-UK firms operating cross-border (without branches) into the United Kingdom are not subject to the same rules (they are subject to the rules in their EU member state of origin, according to the MiFID passporting rules). RDR rules will thus also not apply to investment services provided by UK firms to non-UK resident clients.

All retail investment products, such as funds, personal pensions, life policies, certain closed-ended investment companies, structured capital-at-risk products, investment trusts, individual personal pensions, and other packaged financial products offering exposure to underlying assets, are within the scope of the RDR. But it does not cover individual stocks and bonds, structured deposits, mortgages, and pure protection insurance products. The RDR rules also do not cover execution-only services, so inducements are still payable for products sold without advice.

Reforms in Detail

Under the RDR rules, every retail financial adviser must have a charging structure that will need to be understood and agreed to by the client. Charging structures can range from fixed fee or hourly rate to percentage of amount invested. In addition to upfront charges, ongoing charges are also permissible if the adviser is genuinely performing an ongoing service. The client will also choose whether charges are paid as a separate fee or "facilitated" though a product (that is, deducted from the amount invested in the product). The FCA regards any type of charging structure in which fees vary depending on the provider or the type of product as inappropriate.

Under RDR rules, a product provider must not offer or pay any form of commissions, remunerations, or benefits and must take reasonable steps to ensure a clear distinction between product charges and adviser charges. But a product provider can facilitate adviser charges for advice if it obtains instructions from the retail client.

The RDR also bans payments from product providers to platforms—online services used by intermediaries to view and administer investment portfolios—and requires a platform service to be paid for by a charge that is disclosed to, and agreed on by, the client. Platforms facilitate purchases and sales of investments but are also used by firms to aggregate clients' assets, as well as to arrange their custody.

Standards for Independent vs. Restricted Advice

Under the RDR, before providing advice, advisers must inform clients in writing whether they provide independent or restricted advice (or both). Any advice that is not independent will be labeled as restricted advice—for example, when it relates only to a limited range of products or product providers. In any case, firms are required to fulfill the requirement to act in the best interest of their clients.

Firms providing independent advice are required to make recommendations based on a comprehensive and fair analysis of clients' needs and provide unbiased and unrestricted advice. As a result, independent advisers must consider all retail investment products in the relevant market. They can recommend their own products as long as they consider them against a wider range of products and solutions available.

An advisory firm can be owned (entirely or partially) by a product provider, but this fact should not restrict its recommendations in any way. Firms will need to be able to demonstrate that that they selected a product on the basis of the client's best interests.

Increased Professional Standards

The RDR has also raised the minimum level of qualification for all advisers (whether they provide independent or restricted advice). According to the RDR, advisers need to

- hold an appropriate, modernised qualification, including any qualification gap-fill (structured learning versus exams to fill any qualification gaps);
- adhere to ethical standards;
- carry out at least 35 hours of continuing professional development a year; and
- make an annual declaration that they are meeting standards and as evidence, hold a Statement of Professional Standing (SPS) from an accredited body.

The FCA will maintain, supervise, and enforce a code of ethics, as well as new, enhanced standards for continuing professional development.

Compatibility with EU Regulation (MiFID and MiFID II)

Parts of the RDR regime exceed MiFID requirements and are subject to a notification to the European Commission as stated in Article 4 of MiFID, in which the Commission allows such "gold plating". (Gold plating is "exceeding the requirements of EU legislation when transposing Directives into national law".)

The MiFID II text agreed on in the European Parliament still allows investment firms to be paid fees or commissions by financial product providers or fund managers, except for the provision of advice "on an independent basis". At the same time, it allows individual member states to impose further restrictions on inducements "above and beyond" the minimum standards agreed to at the European level, so the United Kingdom would be able to maintain its complete ban. Similar provisions are included in the latest Council versions of the text, so they are likely to be voted into the final MiFID II text in the next two years.

Creating an "RDR-Ready" Share Class and Treatment of Legacy Assets

For funds, "RDR-ready" share classes must be created that carry a lower management fee (or existing institutional share classes will need to be used) because the investment manager will not have to fund any commission payments from its management fee. Existing "full" management fee share classes are likely to continue in parallel for the foreseeable future, partly related to the fact that the obligation to pay trail commission to the original adviser continues to exist.

The adviser charging rules will only apply to business conducted after the end of 2012. If a client bought a retail investment product before the RDR implementation date, the adviser concerned can continue to receive ongoing "trail" commissions in relation to his or her pre-RDR advice until the product matures or is terminated. The same applies to any pre-agreed, automatic "top-up" investment in that product. But any new advised investment must be made in an "RDR-ready" share class (paying a lower management fee) or benefit from the lack of a commission.

Implications

The tax implications of a ban on commissions should also be addressed. Under current European value added tax (VAT) legislation, the intermediation and distribution of financial products is exempt from VAT, but financial advice is subject to VAT. In the United Kingdom, advice is exempt from VAT when it is provided as part of a broader set of intermediation service provided by an adviser, including recommendations and referrals. When one or more elements of these bundled services (other than the intermediary service) are contracted for separately, the service provided will be subject to VAT. But there is a lack of a common approach to taxes across Europe, so additional clarity is required because any unforeseen charge for VAT will either create an additional cost for investors who want to access the market or, if it cannot be passed on, will reduce the profits of distributors and advisers.

In July 2013, the FCA published the first in a series of planned reviews of the implications of RDR.[20] The review could only cover a short period of time because the RDR only came into effect on 1 January 2013. Even so, the findings were informative. The FCA found that the majority of firms have made progress and there was a willingness to adapt to the new rules.

[20]Financial Conduct Authority (FCA), "Retail Distribution Review Six Months In—How Firms Are Implementing the RDR," Press Release (25 July 2013): www.fca.org.uk/news/rdr-six-months-in.

But there were some reasons for concern:

- Firms providing charges in percentages, rather than cash terms, which some consumers found confusing;
- Firms describing themselves as independent but in fact choosing products from a limited number of providers or products; and
- Firms not clearly explaining what service customers will receive for ongoing fees.

Will most advisers focus more on wealthier customers and leave clients with smaller portfolios behind? Will retail banks do the same and come to the conclusion that it is impractical to offer face-to-face advice to their mass market customers? Both of these prospects seem likely, although the vacuum that is left in the market is likely to be filled by other financial intermediaries, such as bare-bones direct-to-consumer financial firms offering clients the basic infrastructure for managing their own financial accounts with little or no advice.

This expected increase in do-it-yourself investments is supported by a study from the research firm CoreData. The results of the research study indicate that the number of households turning to advisers could shrink by 28% over 20 years. The decline would place downward pressure on the average yearly fees advisers receive, falling from £91,559 for each adviser today to £66,680 in 2033.[21]

Switzerland

Regulator and Inducement Reforms

The Swiss market for financial products is broadly characterised by its predominant reliance on providers' (banks, insurance companies) own distribution channels, which are integrated into a highly automated value chain controlled and operated by the SIX Group, the owner of the stock exchange. Brokers and agents play only a small role in banking products, although their role in the distribution of insurance products is substantial. The role of independent asset managers is significant because they gave rise to the case law that has begun to influence much of the business model of the asset management industry.

[21]CoreData, "Investment Platform Report 2013" (July 2013): www.coredataresearch.co.uk/research/view/investment-platform-report-2013.

Most financial services are governed by the law of mandate ("einfacher Auftrag"), which has been a statute since 1911. Nevertheless, recent case law by the Swiss Federal Court of Justice has begun to overturn the financial services industry's long-standing practice of retaining inducements. The developing case law recognises the retroactive effect. Statutory limitation of claim is set to 10 years.

Reforms in Detail

Based on the Swiss Federal Code of Obligations, Article 400, Paragraph 1, inducements received by a financial intermediary from a third party in connection with the mandate of a client must be passed on to the client. The Swiss Federal Court has repeatedly confirmed its first decision in 2006 in which an asset manager had to pay the inducements obtained from the clients' custodian bank to the client. The court has, however, ruled that a client can validly waive his or her right to claim inducements, provided he or she had been thoroughly and truthfully informed about the details of such payments. In 2011, the Swiss Federal Court further detailed the asset managers' duties to inform clients, including disclosing the estimated size of the payments (calculation basis in percentage ranges) and potential conflicts of interest. In its latest decision in autumn 2012, the Swiss Federal Court confirmed that the disclosure principles also apply to banks that, for example, receive inducements from fund managers for the distribution of their funds.

The Swiss Financial Market Supervisory Authority (FINMA) has recently revised its circular "Guidelines on Asset Management (Eckwerte der Vermögensverwaltung)"[22] to reflect the adoption of these court decisions. Moreover, the Swiss legislature is drafting the new Federal Financial Services Act (Finanzdienstleistungsgesetz). It is not expected to prohibit inducements in the financial market sector but will considerably increase the disclosure and transparency obligations of financial institutions in connection with such inducements.

Implications

Banks quickly revised their titles of claim as well as the terms and conditions imposed on their client base in an attempt to put the business model on a different contractual footing. But when it became evident through subsequent case law that such efforts were doomed, a process of re-thinking the business has started and is still ongoing.

---

[22]Swiss Financial Market Supervisory Authority (FINMA), "Guidelines on Asset Management to Be Revised," Press Release (7 February 2013): www.finma.ch/d/aktuell/seiten/mm-revision-eckwerte-vermoegensverwaltung-rs-09-01-20130207.aspx.

The swiftest response in the marketplace arose from pension funds, which are under close political scrutiny for how they handle the costs of asset management. Sophisticated, large pension funds began to demand immediate, full transparency and refunds of inducements that were not already diminished by the introduction of institutional share classes with little to no management fees. ASIP, the pension fund trade association, highlighted through a series of circulars how pension fund trustees might become liable for negligence if they did not engage their asset managers on the matter.

The response from private clients was notably more subdued. This difference is most likely because of the low intensity of the interactions with a largely offshore client base as well as the difficulty of the subject matter for people not familiar with finance matters. Eventually, though, a small number of activist clients will enforce change, supported by regulators and the lawmakers, who are integrating the case law into their regulatory practice and new laws.

Netherlands

Regulator and Inducement Reforms

Today, almost all Dutch investors receive their financial advice from a few large banks. In the Netherlands, as in the United Kingdom and Australia, investors have long paid for advice through commissions (retrocessions). The Dutch regulator, the Authority on the Financial Markets (AFM), announced in 2011 that it would enforce a "self-regulatory" ban on commissions for the Dutch banks.

Reforms in Detail

On 1 January 2013, the inducement rules for non-MiFID products were amended in the Netherlands by the introduction of a complete ban on third-party inducements. In a similar fashion to that witnessed in the United Kingdom, the Dutch government wanted to break the strong link between the provider of a financial product and the intermediaries and advisers. A ban was believed to be the only way to reach a pure market model whereby the consumer and intermediary (or adviser) determines the reward for the service provided.

The Dutch government banned commissions on financial services products, and in doing so, forced banks and independent advisers to be more transparent about costs. The Dutch have since gone one step further than the RDR and banned commission payments for asset management (which includes professional investors as well as retail), mortgages, and insurance products.

Advisers from banks and independent advisers are subject to the same requirements. Financial advisers who operate on a fee-based model, either an hourly rate or a fixed fee, will be monitored to ensure the cost of the advice service is reasonable. Minimum qualification requirements were introduced for Dutch advisers in 2006, although discussions are taking place about whether this minimum level should be increased further.

Because several aspects of the ban constitute a general standard, the ban has raised many questions for market participants, and recently the AFM provided some additional guidance, such as the following:[23]

- Payment constructions in which the consumer pays the inducements via a surcharge on the interest or premium are not allowed. The consumer must pay the inducements directly to the intermediary or adviser.
- Direct providers are obliged to charge the costs for advice to the consumer to create a level playing field between direct providers and independent intermediaries or advisers.

Other changes proposed by the Dutch minister include a provision for financial service providers that requires them to store data on advice given and financial products sold for a period of five years, as opposed to the current requirement of one year.

The consequence of this extended ban is that investment companies can no longer receive indirect fees (distribution fees, kickback fees, or placement fees) for bringing in new clients.

Implications

These reforms are expected to have a major impact on the Dutch fund industry given that a majority of fund distribution is handled by the banks in the Netherlands. Dutch banks are putting pressure on asset managers to review their fund offerings, and managers need to create share classes that have commission payments stripped out if they want to maintain their lucrative business ties with the large Dutch distributors.

[23]Netherlands Authority for the Financial Markets (AFM), "Tips & Tools" (www.afm.nl/en/consumer/aanpak.aspx).

Italy

Regulator and Inducement Reforms

Inducements in Italy are governed by MiFID. As of October 2013, there is no planned action by the Italian lawmakers to change this framework at the national level. Therefore, inducements are allowed and represent the industry standard.

Lawmakers and Consob, the national regulator, have recently recognised the role of independent financial advisers (IFAs).[24] The national regulation for IFAs, though, still has to be finalised with the constitution of a supervisory entity. This area will likely see further developments in Italy.

Financial advisers need to comply with minimum qualification standards and be registered on official lists. Financial advisers can be tied or independent. Tied advisers sell financial instruments that are distributed by the entity that they are tied to. Most financial advisers' networks in Italy have the flexibility to sell a variety of financial instruments that are not necessarily produced by the entity that they are tied to. This trend toward a "guided open architecture" is also pushed by Consob through regulation, "moral suasion", and specific investigations on potential poor management of conflicts of interest.

Reforms in Detail

Independent financial advisers can also deliver "financial advice". They have to comply with specific laws and regulations (actual independence, minimum levels of education, annual training, etc.) and will only be paid commissions by the client.

IFAs in Italy, however, are still a "work in progress" because the legislature still has to create an official list (albus) and a dedicated supervisory entity that will monitor and legitimise IFAs.

According to the current national law and regulation, "financial advice" is an investment service that can be delivered only by authorised entities (e.g., registered banks or investment firms). When they sell financial instruments, authorised entities and their networks of tied financial advisers can receive inducements according to the current law. But they have to comply with the general principle of "investors' interests" as defined by the MiFID Implementation Directive (2006/73/CE). In particular, Article 26 covers inducements practice and states that

[24]See Consob, Regulation 17130, issued on 12 January 2010: www.consob.it/main/documenti/Regolamentazione/normativa/reg17130.htm (in Italian only).

the payment of the fee or commission, or the provision of the non-monetary benefit must be designed to enhance the quality of the relevant service to the client and not impair compliance with the firm's duty to act in the best interests of the client.

The adoption of MiFID has brought a number of innovations to the Italian market. In this context, it is important to highlight that MiFID allows inducements. But when financial advice is provided, there is an obligation to protect the investors' interest. Depending on the level of financial advice, there is a need to check for appropriateness and suitability.

Suitability

Currently, authorised entities need to obtain from clients or potential clients information that allows the firm to understand essential facts about the client. This information can then be used to create a reasonable basis for believing that the specific transaction to be recommended or entered into satisfies the following criteria found in MiFID:[25]

a. it meets the investment objectives of the client in question;

b. it is such that the client is able financially to bear any related investment risks consistent with his investment objectives;

c. it is such that the client has the necessary experience and knowledge in order to understand the risks involved in the transaction or in the management of his portfolio.

Appropriateness

Authorised entities need to determine whether the client has the necessary experience and knowledge to understand the risks involved in relation to the product or investment service offered or demanded. According to MiFID, financial advisers are required to ask clients to fill in a questionnaire with the aim of determining (1) the client's experience and financial knowledge, (2) her financial situation, and (3) her investment objectives. Although there are no set standards or rules concerning the questionnaire, Consob is responsible for checking that the format and content of questionnaires are compliant with the regulation.

[25]European Commission, "ID 307. Suitability and appropriateness tests (Internal reference 134.) propriety of bank questionnaires" (http://ec.europa.eu/yqol/index.cfm?fuseaction=question.show&questionId=307).

Implications

Under the current regulatory framework, monetary inducements are allowed and represent the industry standard in Italy. Captive distribution models are frequent, which tends to increase possible mis-selling issues. Regulation for independent financial advisers is still partial (in particular, a supervisory entity still has to be finalised), which slows down the development of "fee-only" and open architecture models.

To reduce potential conflicts of interest between investors and intermediaries, some financial institutions moved to a "guided architecture model" under which advisers have multiple alternatives to choose from for the benefit of their clients; this approach seems to be one that many market operators are now looking at adopting.

Some asset managers have also started to offer specific share classes that are dedicated to the direct-to-consumer channel; in fact, when investors decide not to use advisers' services to buy a fund, they might be able to access low-cost share classes.

Germany

Regulator and Inducement Reforms

The Federal Financial Supervisory Authority (BaFin) is the primary financial regulatory authority in Germany. As part of its responsibilities, BaFin oversees banks, financial service companies, insurance companies, and other financial firms.

At this point there has been no full or partial ban on inducements in the German market. It is expected that German authorities will wait for the outcome of MiFID II negotiations before taking any final action on inducements regulation. But BaFin has already started encouraging investors to abandon traditional distribution channels and adopt fee-based independent advice.[26]

Starting in 2013, all German investment service providers are required to record in a "list of inducements" any fees, commissions, or other monetary or non-monetary inducements that they receive in relation to providing an investment or ancillary service to clients.

[26]David Ricketts, "Netherlands Edging Closer to RDR-Style Reform," *Ignites Europe*, a *Financial Times* publication (10 April 2013): www.ft.com/intl/cms/s/0/1ba97e5a-a1dc-11e2-ad0c-00144feabdc0.html.

Reforms in Detail

There are concerns that a ban on inducements could harm the business of asset managers—put the asset management business model at risk and put many independent advisers out of work. The BVI, Germany's fund association, said recently that a potential ban on retrocession fees in Germany would be a "horror scenario".[27]

There has been no full or partial ban on inducements and there is no serious talk of such a step by BaFin. What there has been in the interim is increased transparency. Regulators have called for firms to disclose all inducements from the distributor side.

Starting at the beginning of 2013, each financial firm must create a database of all inducement agreements in which that firm is involved.[28] Each firm will have to list these inducements and report them at the end of the firm's calendar year. The list of inducements must distinguish between monetary and non-monetary inducements. The list of inducements can be set up in writing or electronically. The firm must also detail how it has spent the monetary inducements to enhance the services it provides its clients.

This year is the first year the inducements list is in place (2013), so we should start seeing these reports at the end of 2013. The format of disclosure is up to each firm—there is no uniform format for these reports.

Implications

There is no expectation of a ban on inducements in Germany at this point, although regulators are expected to wait until the conclusion of MiFID II negotiations before making a final decision on inducement regulation. Like their counterparts in the majority of European markets, German regulators are vying first for increased transparency around inducements while keenly watching the ramifications of bans on inducements in the United Kingdom and the Netherlands.

[27]David Ricketts, "Netherlands Edging Closer to RDR-Style Reform," *Ignites Europe*, a *Financial Times* publication (10 April 2013): www.ft.com/intl/cms/s/0/1ba97e5a-a1dc-11e2-ad0c-00144feabdc0.html.
[28]Euro Fund Research, "BaFin: Berater Müssen Zuwendungen Dokumentieren" (17 January 2013): www.fundresearch.de/Nachrichten/Top-Themen/Bafin-Berater-muessen-Zuwendungen-dokumentieren.html (in German only).

France

Regulator and Inducement Reforms

In France, inducements on financial instruments must abide by the MiFID legislation. In mid-2013, the Financial Markets Authority (AMF) issued a consultation on compensation and benefits received in connection with the marketing and portfolio management of financial instruments.[29]

In the consultation, AMF emphasised the need for clients to be made aware of any fee or commission they are paying and also be given enough information to link any fee to the service for which the fee is paid.

Reforms in Detail

The AMF consultation document details recommendations regarding remuneration and benefits received in connection with the marketing and management of mandated financial instruments.

The AMF recommendations stipulate that a financial investment adviser is regarded as acting honestly, fairly, and professionally in accordance with the best interests of a client if that adviser receives compensation or commission or provides or receives a non-monetary benefit following a fee or commission paid by the customer when

a. the customer is clearly informed of the existence, nature, and amount of the fee, commission, or benefit, or if the amount cannot be ascertained, the method of calculation. This information is comprehensive, accurate, and understandable before the advisory service is provided. The financial investment adviser may disclose the essential terms of the agreements on salaries, commissions, or non-monetary benefits in summary form, provided it agrees to provide further details at the request of the client and that it fulfills this commitment; or

b. the payment of the fee or commission, or the provision of the non-monetary benefit, is to improve the quality of consulting services provided to the client and must not interfere with the fulfillment of the obligation the financial investment adviser to act in the best interests of the client.

[29]See the website for Autorité des Marchés Financiers (AMF): www.amf-france.org.

The AMF considers remunerations received "over time" as legitimate only in cases when the client is provided with an increase in service over the same period as remunerations are received; this increase must include meeting with the client

- at least annually,
- in a personalised manner (i.e., information should not be limited to generic information),
- following a schedule pre-defined with the client when initially granting investment advice, and
- to ensure the product initially suggested is still adapted (the product's risk profile may have varied over time) to the client (the client's profile may have varied over time).

Implications

As in most European markets, there is no plan for a ban on inducements in France at this time. The AMF postponed decisions on inducements in the case of discretionary portfolio management and currently seems content in their call for greater transparency as a safeguard for the interests of French investors.

Spain

Regulator and Inducement Reforms

One of the most prominent cases of mis-selling in Europe over the last few years is the widespread sale of hybrid products by banks to small retail investors in Spain. These hybrids, commonly sold under the name participaciones preferentes (preference shares), offered high nominal returns but only as long as the balance sheet of the bank remained healthy. During the real estate and financial crisis, as the capital position of banks deteriorated, returns froze and any illusion of liquidity dissipated. When the European Union implemented its rescue scheme for the Spanish financial sector, preference shares were converted into equity with haircuts of up to 70% of their nominal value, not including the subsequent volatility of share prices in the stock market.

It is estimated that roughly 400,000 retail clients purchased these hybrids between 2008 and 2011, with a nominal value in excess of €12.5 billion. Some financial institutions actively sought their retail clients through their local branches, relying on long-standing relationships of trust. The deepening of the eurozone crisis made those relationships burst, leading to massive losses.

The Spanish Securities Market Commission (CNMV) initiated actions for a range of violations of MiFID. The most common violation relates to the incorrect application of the suitability and appropriateness assessments, followed by the inadequate management of conflicts of interest, and lastly, the provision of erroneous or misleading information. The extent of the violations is still to be determined. A special arbitration procedure has so far permitted 50% of retail investors to recover all or most of the money lost.

Reforms in Detail

In reviewing its policy for the sale of complex financial products to retail investors, the Spanish supervisor has requested greater authority to intervene, broader operational capabilities, and the ability to issue higher sanctions. It has also introduced guidelines requiring clients to spell out their acknowledgement of advice received in the document of purchase. For instance, when a complex product is purchased against a negative recommendation of the financial adviser, the investor would have to spell out—in his or her own handwriting and next to his or her signature—"This product is complex and is considered as not suitable for me".

Implications

There is currently no talk of inducement bans in Spain. Spain will in the future have to implement MiFID II, so investors will be presented with the distinction between independent and inducements-based advice.

In Spain, management fees have a maximum limit. The CNMV stipulates that any retrocessions received by a management company must be for the express benefit of collective investment schemes (CIS) and the shareholders, and they cannot be received by the management companies of those undertakings. Such an approach does not currently apply to investment advisers, but it may be a preview of the direction regulation in Spain may be headed.

National Examples—Asia Pacific

Survey respondents in Asia Pacific largely agree with their global counterparts concerning the reforms most needed to combat mis-selling, although CFA Institute members in APAC believe that reforming pay structures at distributors is more important (65%) than mandating full disclosure of product costs (55%), whereas global survey respondents put the importance of these steps in the reverse order, with mandating full disclosure as the most important reform, as shown in **Table 10**.

Table 10. What are the most important reforms needed to combat mis-selling?

	Total	APAC
Reforming pay structures at distributors, linking staff and senior management remuneration to good investment outcomes for clients	56%	65%
Completely banning commission payments by product producers	15%	13%
Reforming commission payment structures by product producers (to reduce incentives to favor unsuitable products), while retaining them at least partially	35%	43%
Requiring a minimum standard of professional qualifications	43%	43%
Requiring wider product offerings by all distributors	5%	4%
Improving disclosure of product information to clients	46%	47%
Mandating full disclosure of product cost structures to clients	65%	55%
Mandating clear disclosure of all commission payments received by distributors before investment	60%	55%
Improving redress possibilities for clients (in particular retail clients)	24%	25%
Improving enforcement by national regulators	23%	27%
Improving investor education	46%	48%
Other	6%	5%
No Opinion	1%	1%
Unweighted Sample Size	514	91

The opinions of CFA Institute's APAC members do not differ materially from their global cohorts when assessing the main causes of mis-selling, as both think that inappropriate internal remuneration structures at distributors is the main identifiable cause. Survey respondents in APAC are slightly more likely to identify inappropriate commission payments by product producers as a main cause of mis-selling, but both those in APAC and around the world rank this cause as the third most prevalent cause of mis-selling (see **Table 11**).

Table 11. In your opinion, what are the main causes of mis-selling?

	Total	APAC
Inappropriate commission payments by product producers	48%	55%
Inappropriate internal remuneration structures at distributors (skewed toward volume sales or specific products)	70%	75%
Selling pressure from other internal group entities	63%	65%
Lack of professional qualifications	32%	31%
Lack of transparency regarding product comparisons	36%	31%
Laziness	19%	11%
Other	6%	8%
No opinion	2%	1%
Unweighted Sample Size	514	91

APAC members were far more concerned than their global counterparts that small clients would not be able to afford advice and that distributors would stop offering some products altogether. The also appeared relatively more concerned than global members that small distributors would go out of business if commissions were banned, as shown in **Table 12.**

Table 12. If commission payments by product producers are banned completely, what consequences, if any, do you see occurring as a result?

	Total	APAC
Distributors will stop offering particular products altogether, so product choice will diminish.	30%	42%
Retail clients will refuse to pay fees for advice.	16%	21%
Small retail clients will not be able to afford advice.	29%	43%
Distributors will continue to offer advice, but will shrink the product offerings to those they continue to receive fees on.	46%	42%
Distributors will continue to offer advice, but will offer only "in-house" products (products from their own financial group).	38%	32%
Banks will stop offering advice altogether, and will steer client money into deposits.	12%	23%
Small distributors will go out of business, reducing distribution channel choice and reducing product and service choice.	25%	35%
Other	12%	10%
None—I don't see any consequences of a complete ban of commission payments by product producers.	12%	5%
No opinion	6%	4%
Unweighted Sample Size	513	91

Barring a complete ban on commissions, survey respondents in APAC agreed with their colleagues around the globe that introducing clear standards for cost disclosures in the same way as there are standards for performance disclosure is the best option for reform (see **Table 13**). Those in APAC are much more likely to endorse revising commission structures than their global counterparts (58% versus 45%, respectively).

Table 13. How, if at all, could commission payments by product producers be reformed without a complete ban?

	Total	APAC
Revising commission structures to eliminate those that encourage volume sales (tiered commissions)	45%	58%
Providing only for minimum remuneration levels to compensate for distribution expenses incurred	17%	15%
Setting equal commission levels (as a fixed percentage of the management fee) for all products in the same category	32%	24%
Introducing clear standards for cost disclosures in the same way as there are standards for performance disclosure	68%	62%
Other	7%	8%
No opinion	5%	5%
Unweighted Sample Size	511	91

Table 14 shows that survey respondents in APAC appear to be slightly more concerned than their global peers about the loss of distribution channels and reduction of product range by distributors if a ban on commissions comes to pass in their market.

Table 14. How serious do you consider the potential loss of distribution channels and/or the reduction of product range by distributors in case of restrictions or bans on commission payments?

	Total	APAC
1 - Not serious at all	18%	10%
2	17%	9%
3	21%	21%
4	22%	29%
5 - Very serious	16%	24%
No opinion	6%	8%
Unweighted Sample Size	513	91

Australia

Regulator and Inducement Reforms:

A ban on conflicted remuneration was instituted in 2012 as part of the Future of Financial Advice (FOFA) reforms and applies to both personal and general advice given to retail clients about any financial product, including managed investments, superannuation, and platforms. The ban applies to commissions, volume-based payments, soft dollar benefits, and volume-based shelf space fees.

The Corporations Amendment (FOFA) Act of 2012[30] and the Corporations Amendment (Further Future of Financial Advice Measures) Act of 2012, collectively called the "FOFA Acts", amended the Corporations Act of 2001 to implement the FOFA reforms.[31] The acts commenced on 1 July 2012. Compliance with the new measures was voluntary until 1 July 2013 and then compliance became mandatory.

Reforms in Detail

The reforms are intended to improve the trust and confidence of Australian retail investors in the financial planning sector, and they are designed to address conflicts of interest that have threatened the quality of financial advice given to Australian investors.

The Future of Financial Advice package includes the following:[32]

- *A prospective ban on conflicted remuneration structures, including commissions*, in relation to the distribution of and advice on retail investment products, including managed investments, superannuation, and margin loans.
- The introduction of a *statutory fiduciary duty, mandating that financial advisers act in the best interests of their clients*, subject to a "reasonable steps" qualification, and to place the best interests of their clients ahead of their own when providing personal advice to retail clients.

[30]Australian Government, "Corporations Amendment (Future of Financial Advice) Act 2012," ComLaw (www.comlaw.gov.au/Details/C2012A00067).
[31]Australian Government, "Corporations Amendment (Further Future of Financial Advice Measures) Act 2012," ComLaw (www.comlaw.gov.au/Details/C2012A00068).
[32]Treasury, Australian Government, "Future of Financial Advice: The Reforms" (April 2011): http://futureofadvice.treasury.gov.au/content/Content.aspx?doc=reforms.htm.

- Increasing transparency and flexibility of payments for financial advice by introducing a *twice-yearly opt-in arrangement* ensuring that consumers are more engaged with their financial advice services, and annual fee disclosure statements will provide consumers with transparency about the ongoing fees they pay.

- *Percentage-based fees* (known as assets under management fees) will be charged only on ungeared products or investment amounts and only if this arrangement is agreed to by the retail investor.

- *Expanding the availability of low-cost "simple advice"* to improve access to and affordability of financial advice.

- Strengthening the powers of the Australian Securities and Investments Commission to act against unscrupulous operators.

- The examination of the need for a *statutory compensation scheme* for financial services.

The FOFA reforms introduce a ban on conflicted remuneration. Advisers will not be allowed to give or receive payments or non-monetary benefits that could reasonably be expected to influence financial product recommendations or financial product advice provided to retail clients. The ban is principles-based, so the ability of a payment to influence advice matters rather than the structure of a payment.

The ban applies to general advice (advice on products not tailored to an individual's personal circumstances) and personal advice. Commissions being paid by product manufacturers to financial advisers in relation to existing investments can continue to be paid after the reforms commence.

The ban on soft-dollar benefits is not intended to cover the services provided by an employer to its employee advisers. Such services as training and technical support, which are provided by a licensee to its representatives and employees, are unlikely to be prohibited because they are deemed to be unlikely to influence the advice clients receive.

Advisers will not have to comply with the opt-in requirements if they are bound by an approved code of conduct that achieves the same objective as opt-in.

Implications

The inducement reforms will change the way financial advice is provided. In the near term, FOFA will test the role that commissions play in adviser recommendations. If investment activity declines without inducements, the profit margins and health of advisers are likely to suffer.

The ban on commissions in Australia will force clients and advisers to adapt to a fee-only model—some blend of assets under management fees, retainer fees, or even hourly fees (which appear to have almost no presence in Australia yet).

As in the United Kingdom, there are currently very few direct-to-consumer or low-cost/low-service investment options in Australia. These models are likely to proliferate in Australia in the coming years and offer low-advice/low-cost alternatives for investing. There are concerns that this may result in aggressive direct-to-consumer financial products advertising that leads to many instances of inappropriate investments being sold to retail clients. Only time will tell.

Soon after the FOFA reforms became mandatory, the Australian Securities and Investment Commission released Report 362, which reviews the practices of financial advisers.[33] Although at the time of the report the FOFA reforms had only been mandatory for a month, the report found that the majority of advisers' remunerations were still received from product issuers, or commission-based payment.

Although many types of commissions were banned under the government's FOFA reforms, grandfathered commissions (trail commissions) and commissions on some insurance products are still allowed. Also, one unintended consequence of the FOFA reforms may be that advisers are encouraged to stay with the firm they are currently working for so they can keep their grandfather status and thus their trail commissions. If an adviser moves to a new firm, they would no longer receive the trail commissions. This consequence may cause an artificial lack of movement in the industry that may negatively limit the pursuit of new clients and thus limit competition.

[33]Australian Securities and Investments Commission (ASIC), Report 362 "Review of Financial Advice Industry Practice: Phase 2" (July 2013): www.asic.gov.au/asic/pdflib.nsf/LookupByFileName/rep362-published-31-July-2013.pdf/$file/rep362-published-31-July-2013.pdf.

Hong Kong

Regulator and Inducement Reforms

In May 2013, the Hong Kong Federation of Insurers (HKFI) issued new guidance to the life insurance industry that introduced measures aimed at increasing transparency and customer protection. The new rule applies only to financial advisers selling investment-linked insurance products in Hong Kong.

Financial advisers selling investment-linked assurance schemes (ILAS) in Hong Kong will have to formally disclose commissions to their clients in a newly created important facts statement (IFS) starting 1 July 2013. This disclosure has to be followed by a call from the life insurance company confirming that the adviser's remuneration has been properly explained.

Reforms in Detail

The Office of the Commissioner of Insurance, the Hong Kong Monetary Authority, the Securities and Futures Commission, and the HKFI cooperated on producing new rules calling on financial advisers that offer ILAS to formally disclose commission payments to their clients.

Another of the new consumer protection measures is a requirement that life insurance companies must contact each client after the purchase of an ILAS to ensure that they understand the product fully and understand the adviser's remuneration. Although such a checkup on clients is encouraging, it is unclear from the regulation just how rigorous such a process is required to be to confirm a client's level of understanding.

The advisory process has to incorporate a needs analysis and risk profile questionnaire and an IFS. The IFS includes a "statement that explains that remuneration will be payable" and that "insurers and their agents should disclose at least the basic commission rates".

Investment-linked assurance schemes are common pension plans sold by banks and financial advisers to individuals. Historically, insurance firms include fees in the schemes to pay the agents and brokers a commission. Regulators are concerned that this creates a strong incentive to sell a plan regardless of whether the plan is in an investor's best interest.

But there are loopholes in the rules. Most investors who buy such schemes buy investment-linked products through a bank. Sales staff in banks are not insurance brokers and are thus not covered by the new disclosure rule and are under no requirement to disclose fee income to customers in banks.

The new rules require brokers to reveal their full commission on insurance sales, *if* a client asks. So, it is up to the client to know enough to ask for such disclosure.

All these rules will increase transparency of ILAS fees, but the reforms cover only the Hong Kong insurance industry and even then are not as far reaching as some would like.

Under the new rules, brokers must disclose fees on insurance sales only if it is higher than that "customarily paid".

Implications

The focus in Hong Kong is currently on better disclosure around commission payments for only one financial product—ILAS. Commission disclosure rules covering all advisers and all financial products are not currently on the table. A ban on commissions is unlikely in the near future.

India

Regulator and Inducement Reforms

The Securities and Exchange Board of India (SEBI) is the securities regulator in India. SEBI drafts regulations in its legislative capacity, undertakes investigation and enforcement action in its executive function, and passes rulings and orders in its judicial capacity.

After a number of mis-selling abuses during the 2004–07 bull market, in 2009, SEBI banned payment of any kind of entry load on mutual funds in India.

SEBI published draft guideline for advisor regulation in 2012 in the "Concept Paper on Regulation of Investment Advisors". This regulation went into effect on 20 April 2013.

Reforms in Detail

In India, the product distribution space contains conflicts between the manufacturers of financial products, such as banks, mutual funds, and insurance companies, and the distributors that sell these products (agents, financial advisers, financial planners, etc.).

According to SEBI, two major conflicts of interest in the financial product distribution space are the following:

1. The dual role played by distributors as an agent of the investors as well as of the manufacturers. This arrangement is related to the fact that with many financial products, agents receive their payments from two sources: commissions from the manufacturers (either directly or through deductions from the investment amount of investors) and advisory fees or other charges from the investors.

2. A situation might arise in which distributors are likely to be partial to, and would sell more products of, the manufacturer who is the best paymaster; ultimately, other manufacturers would scramble to do the same, thus leading to a race to the bottom.

Starting in August 2009, SEBI banned entry loads on mutual fund investments and mandated that upfront commissions should be paid by the investors directly to the distributors based on certain factors, such as an assessment of the service of the distributor. But the distributor continued to earn trail commissions from the asset management company at the same time. Thus, the first conflict of interest was only partially mitigated in this model.

According to the new law, "no financial incentives/consideration would be received from any person other than investors seeking advice." This mandate is intended to move the market to a client pays model for the investment advice, which bases the payment on the value that the client derives from the adviser.

There could be many possible solutions to conflicts of interest issues, including enhanced disclosures. But in a country like India with low levels of literacy and even lower financial literacy, disclosures have a limited effect.

To resolve the conflicts of interest listed earlier, SEBI suggests the following:

1. People who interface with the customer should declare upfront whether they are financial advisers or agents of the manufacturer.

2. If they are advisers, they would be subject to the regulation of investment advisers presented in the concept paper and would require a much higher level of qualifications. They would act as an adviser to the investor on all financial products. They would also receive all payments from the investor and there would be no limits set on these payments. For those agents who are associated with the manufacturer, they would receive their remuneration from them. But they will be prevented from styling themselves as financial advisers and will have to call themselves "agents only".

SEBI plans to set up a self-regulatory organization (SRO) to implement these rules and take punitive action when necessary. The SRO will need to monitor the activities of a large number of entities, so it is too early to tell whether this organisation will have the resources to be an effective enforcer of regulation. As of this writing (October 2013), no such SRO has been established in India, although SEBI is said to be close to picking an SRO for the job.[34]

Implications

Although there have certainly been cases of mis-selling in recent years, incentives for aggressively churning investor portfolios have been reduced after SEBI's move to ban entry loads in 2009. Some manufacturers of financial products may be trying to influence product sales by offering better commissions. But a race to the bottom may be mitigated by SEBI's control of the expense ratios for some manufacturers of financial products.

SEBI should ensure that the SRO proposed to monitor compliance with the new regulations has the requisite authority to implement the rules and also take enforcement action against advisers who break the rules.

The mutual fund industry is in a nascent stage in India, so there will likely be growing pains. India currently has no plans for across-the-board bans on adviser commissions that are on the same level as those in the United Kingdom and Australia.

Singapore

Regulator and Inducement Reforms

Early in 2013, the Singapore Financial Advisory Industry Review (FAIR) panel rejected a complete ban on commissions for financial advisers. The panel's report on recommendations for changes to the financial advisory industry aimed to raise the competence of financial advisers, raise the quality of advisory firms, make financial advisory a dedicated service, lower costs to investors, and promote a culture of fair dealing. The Monetary Authority

[34]*Times of India*, "Sebi to Appoint SRO for Mutual Fund Distributors Soon" (6 October 2013): http://articles.timesofindia.indiatimes.com/2013-10-06/india-business/42763244_1_mutual-fund-distributors-sro-self-regulatory-organisation.

of Singapore (MAS) reviewed the recommendations and reached a final decision on the recommendations in September, agreeing with most of the FAIR panel recommendations, rejecting only one of them.[35]

The FAIR panel was formed in 2012 with the mission of improving standards in the financial advisory industry. An online survey of consumers in Singapore about their receptiveness of a fee-based model revealed that 80% of consumers were not prepared to pay an upfront fee for advice.

Reforms in Detail

MAS conducted a mystery shopping exercise at the end of 2011 that revealed that 30% of the products recommended to investors in Singapore were unsuitable and that Singaporeans did not adequately plan their finances. Singaporeans were underinsured by about 3.7 times their annual income, and 4 out of 10 people in Singapore did not plan for their retirement or for other contingencies. The FAIR panel, after eight months of intense deliberations, released a series of recommendations under five main focus areas:[36]

1. Raise the competence level of financial advisory representatives through minimum entry requirements and continuing professional development.

2. Raise the quality of financial advisory firms through enhanced requirements on minimum base capital, continuing financial resources, professional indemnity insurance, and dedicated compliance arrangements.

3. Make financial advising a dedicated service by recruiting representatives whose professional focus is primarily on their advisory role with no conflicts of interest with their business as well as better accountability and disclosure to customers.

4. Lower distribution costs by harnessing competitive market forces rather than banning commissions.

[35]Monetary Authority of Singapore, "Response to Feedback Received – Public Consultation on Recommendations of the Financial Advisory Industry Review" (September 2013): www.mas.gov.sg/~/media/MAS/News%20and%20Publications/Consultation%20Papers/Response%20to%20Feedback%20Received%20on%20Public%20Consultation%20on%20Recommendations%20of%20the%20Financial%20Advisory%20Industry%20Review.pdf.

[36]Monetary Authority of Singapore (MAS), "Report on Recommendations of the Financial Advisory Industry Review Panel" (16 January 2013): www.mas.gov.sg/~/media/resource/news_room/press_releases/2013/Annex%201%20%20Report%20on%20recommendations%20of%20the%20Financial%20Advisory%20Industry%20Review%20Panel.pdf.

5. Promote a culture of fair dealing by requiring all financial advisory firms to adopt a balanced scorecard framework and ban all product-specific incentives.

FAIR proposed a more even distribution of total commissions paid on life insurance products, with no more than 40% of commissions paid in the first year. The panel recommended that financial advisory firms adopt a balanced scorecard approach that incorporates non-sales performance criteria for advisers, such as the quality of advice and suitability of recommendations. The panel also calls for the ban of all product-specific incentives.

The panel recommended the creation of an online platform that allows consumers to compare the pricing and benefits of similar insurance products offered by different companies. The panel recommends that life insurance companies provide a direct channel for self-directed customers to buy basic insurance products from the insurer for a nominal fee.

Recommendations also include higher educational requirements for financial advisers.

Implications

The reforms in Singapore focus on transparency and building trust in the financial adviser industry. A banning of commissions was considered by the FAIR panel but ultimately rejected in favor of letting market forces do the work of reform.

According to the FAIR report:

> The Panel considered capping or abolishing commissions as a way to reduce costs of life insurance products to consumers. Whilst these approaches may have their merits, the Panel is mindful of possible unintended consequences. Jurisdictions that employ commission caps, such as New York and Malaysia, have observed price rigidity, as commissions gravitate to and remain at the caps. Singapore experienced the same before caps on commissions were removed in 2002. After the caps were removed, distribution costs for products, such as whole life policies, trended lower.... An even more radical idea is to abolish commissions entirely and move to a 'fee-only' model. While the United Kingdom and Australia have adopted this model, it may be premature to impose a 'fee-only' model in the Singapore market. From a survey conducted by MAS, 80% of the respondents indicated that they would not pay a fee for financial advice. Thus, a 'fee-only' model may result in more Singaporeans being under-advised or under-insured. It is also not clear that fees will be lower than commissions. Indeed, it is possible that consumers may end up paying more (pages 17–18).

National Examples—Americas

There has been little talk of commission bans in either the United States or Canada, with efforts to combat mis-selling mostly focusing on increased transparency and the fiduciary duty owed to clients by their financial advisers.

There is little difference of opinion between global survey respondents and those from the Americas (primarily the United States and Canada) concerning the most needed mis-selling reforms. Both groups believe that mandating full disclosure of product cost structures and clear disclosure of all commission payments are the most important reforms, as shown in **Table 15**.

Table 15. **What are the most important reforms needed to combat mis-selling?**

	Total	Americas
Reforming pay structures at distributors, linking staff and senior management remuneration to good investment outcomes for clients	56%	54%
Completely banning commission payments by product producers	15%	15%
Reforming commission payment structures by product producers (to reduce incentives to favor unsuitable products), while retaining them at least partially	35%	34%
Requiring a minimum standard of professional qualifications	43%	41%
Requiring wider product offerings by all distributors	5%	5%
Improving disclosure of product information to clients	46%	44%
Mandating full disclosure of product cost structures to clients	65%	68%
Mandating clear disclosure of all commission payments received by distributors before investment	60%	64%
Improving redress possibilities for clients (in particular retail clients)	24%	22%
Improving enforcement by national regulators	23%	22%
Improving investor education	46%	44%
Other	6%	6%
No Opinion	1%	1%
Unweighted Sample Size	514	158

The opinions of CFA Institute members in the Americas do not differ much from their global colleagues when assessing the main causes of mis-selling, as both think that inappropriate internal remuneration structures at distributors and selling pressures from other internal groups are the most identifiable causes (see **Table 16**).

Table 16. In your opinion, what are the main causes of mis-selling?

	Total	Americas
Inappropriate commission payments by product producers	48%	48%
Inappropriate internal remuneration structures at distributors (skewed toward volume sales or specific products)	70%	68%
Selling pressure from other internal group entities	63%	63%
Lack of professional qualifications	32%	30%
Lack of transparency regarding product comparisons	36%	37%
Laziness	19%	23%
Other	6%	6%
No opinion	2%	3%
Unweighted Sample Size	514	158

Survey respondents in the Americas agree with their global counterparts that the most likely result of a commission ban would be a decrease in product offerings from distributors and more focus on "in house" products from distributors. Those in the Americas tend to be less concerned that distributors will stop offering particular products altogether or that retail clients will refuse to pay fees for advice than do survey respondents in other regions, as **Table 17** shows.

Table 17. If commission payments by product producers are banned completely, what consequences, if any, do you see occurring as a result?

	Total	Americas
Distributors will stop offering particular products altogether, so product choice will diminish.	30%	25%
Retail clients will refuse to pay fees for advice.	16%	10%
Small retail clients will not be able to afford advice.	29%	24%
Distributors will continue to offer advice, but will shrink the product offerings to those they continue to receive fees on.	46%	47%
Distributors will continue to offer advice, but will offer only "in-house" products (products from their own financial group).	38%	38%
Banks will stop offering advice altogether, and will steer client money into deposits.	12%	8%
Small distributors will go out of business, reducing distribution channel choice and reducing product and service choice.	25%	19%
Other	12%	13%
None—I don't see any consequences of a complete ban of commission payments by product producers.	12%	15%
No opinion	6%	6%
Unweighted Sample Size	513	157

Like their colleagues around the globe, survey respondents in the Americas tended to favour introducing a clear standard for cost disclosures and revising commission structures as the most effective ways to combat mis-selling without a complete ban on commissions (see **Table 18**).

Table 18. How, if at all, could commission payments by product producers be reformed without a complete ban?

	Total	Americas
Revising commission structures to eliminate those that encourage volume sales (tiered commissions)	45%	41%
Providing only for minimum remuneration levels to compensate for distribution expenses incurred	17%	18%
Setting equal commission levels (as a fixed percentage of the management fee) for all products in the same category	32%	35%
Introducing clear standards for cost disclosures in the same way as there are standards for performance disclosure	68%	68%
Other	7%	8%
No opinion	5%	5%
Unweighted Sample Size	511	157

Assuming a hypothetical ban on commissions, survey respondents in the Americas tended to be less concerned about the loss of distribution channels and reduction of product range by distributors than their global counterparts, as shown in **Table 19**.

Table 19. How serious do you consider the potential loss of distribution channels and/or the reduction of product range by distributors in case of restrictions or bans on commission payments?

	Total	Americas
1 - Not serious at all	18%	22%
2	17%	19%
3	21%	22%
4	22%	18%
5 - Very serious	16%	13%
No opinion	6%	8%
Unweighted Sample Size	513	157

Canada

Regulator and Inducement Reforms

Under the registration regime in Canada, persons or companies can be registered under securities legislation as advisers, dealers, and/or investment fund managers, depending on the nature of their activities. In general terms, only advisers and dealers can provide advice on investing in securities.

The standard of conduct applicable to registrants is defined by reference to a number of different securities legislation requirements. Advisers and dealers that are members of a self-regulatory organisation are also subject to the separate rules of the SRO that apply to them.

In October 2012, the Canadian Securities Administrators (CSA) published for comment the CSA Consultation Paper 33-403, "The Standard of Conduct for Advisers and Dealers: Exploring the Appropriateness of Introducing a Statutory Best Interest Duty When Advice is Provided to Retail Clients". The consultation paper explores the potential benefits and competing considerations of introducing a statutory fiduciary, or best interest, standard for advisers and dealers when they provide advice to retail clients. A ban on commissions is not seen as likely.

Four provinces (Alberta, Manitoba, Newfoundland and Labrador, and New Brunswick) have a statutory requirement that when advisers or dealers have discretionary authority over their clients' investments, the advisers or dealers must act in the clients' best interests.

In Québec, according to both the general civil law and the Securities Act (Québec), registered dealers and advisers are currently subject to a duty of loyalty and a duty of care and must act in the client's best interest.

Reforms in Detail

CSA staff are considering the introduction of a statutory best interest standard for advisers and dealers when providing investment advice to retail investors. For consultation purposes, one possible articulation of this standard would be as follows:

Every adviser and dealer (and each of their representatives) that provides advice to a retail client with respect to investing in, buying, or selling securities or derivatives shall, when providing such advice,

1. act in the best interests of the retail client, and

2. exercise the degree of care, diligence, and skill that a reasonably prudent person or company would exercise in the circumstances.

Although other statutory best interest duties already exist in certain CSA jurisdictions, as in Québec, the CSA is exploring the possibility of harmonising the appropriate standard of conduct for advisers and dealers that should apply across Canada. If such a new harmonised standard of conduct for advisers and dealers in Canada is identified by the CSA, further work would be needed to reflect it appropriately in each CSA jurisdiction.

No decision has been made yet about whether a statutory best interest standard should be adopted, whether another policy solution is preferable, or whether the current regulatory regime is adequate.

Implications

The CSA is not currently considering a ban on commissions as a way to combat mis-selling, focusing instead on standards of transparency and attempting to harmonise an understanding of what fiduciary duty an adviser owes to his or her client. None of the Canadian provinces are considering a commission ban at this time.

United States

Regulator and Inducement Reforms

There has been no talk in the United States of limiting commissions as a way to increase the accountability of financial advisers. The focus instead has been on the issue of fiduciary duty, the definition of fiduciary duty, and what duty is ultimately owed to clients serviced by a number of different individuals, from registered advisers to broker dealers.

Although the US Dodd–Frank Act gave the US Securities and Exchange Commission (SEC) authority to create a regulation that would impose a uniform fiduciary standard of care for retail investment advice, and a January 2011 SEC report recommended that the agency proceed with a rule, the agency has not taken action as of this report. The SEC is currently conducting a cost–benefit analysis of changing the fiduciary duty standard.

Section 913 of the Dodd–Frank Act states that the commission model has to be accommodated in any new rulemaking,[37] which makes it highly unlikely that a ban on commissions would happen in the United States without new legislation.

The SEC, however, recently took a step toward a possible implementation by seeking input on the duties of brokers, dealers, and investment advisers.[38] The SEC's request comes after past court challenges led ultimately to other SEC regulatory initiatives being overturned.

There is a need for clarity in the relationship between an investor and his adviser and what that investor is getting and being charged. A recent study by research firm Cerulli Associates found that investors rarely understand how their advisers are paid. One-third of those surveyed said they were not sure how they paid for the advice they received, and 29% said the services were free. The adviser often does not have an incentive to make this information clear to clients and investors often do not understand how compensation is imbedded in the products they buy.

Reforms in Detail

Currently in the United States, advisers' obligations to their clients depend on whether they are registered with the Financial Industry Regulatory Authority (FINRA) or the SEC.

FINRA-registered advisers—"registered representatives" of securities firms—typically are paid with commissions when investors buy or sell securities. Advisers who charge fees for advice generally are registered investment advisers (RIAs), overseen by either the SEC or state securities regulators. Many financial professionals may be regulated by both FINRA and the SEC, each for a different part of their business. Investors may, therefore, pay the same individual both an advisory fee and trading commissions.

Advisers who charge commissions are required to make sure a product is *appropriate* for an investor before selling it, but RIAs are held to a higher standard—a fiduciary standard. This higher standard means that RIAs have an obligation to think about what investments would *best serve* the client. Fee-only advisers are paid only by their clients, and thus in theory they have no incentive to favor a particular financial product to sell to their clients. Investors can file arbitration claims or request mediation through FINRA when they have disputes with a brokerage firm or one of its brokers.

[37]US SEC, "Study on Investment Advisers and Broker–Dealers" (January 2011): www.sec.gov/news/studies/2011/913studyfinal.pdf.

[38]US SEC, "Duties of Brokers, Dealers, and Investment Advisers," Release No. 34-69013 (2013): www.sec.gov/rules/other/2013/34-69013.pdf.

The SEC is currently requesting data relating to the benefits and costs that could result from various alternative approaches regarding the standards of conduct and other obligations of broker/dealers and investment advisers (fiduciary duty). The feedback the SEC receives will inform their consideration of alternative standards of conduct for broker/dealers and investment advisers when providing personalised investment advice about securities to retail customers. The US Department of Labor (DOL), which makes the rules concerning labor pension funds, is also considering changes to its definition of fiduciary duty. There have been calls for the SEC and the DOL to work together so that they do not come up with two different interpretations of fiduciary duty in the United States.

Implications

Whatever fiduciary standard is decided on by the SEC will have large ramifications for investors in the US market because the duty owed to investors by their advisers or brokers may change. But changes to the commissions structure is not on the regulatory agenda at this time.

Investor Protection Alternatives to Bans on Inducements—Efficacy

Most markets around the world have chosen to forgo a ban on inducements in favor of some form of increased transparency to combat mis-selling in the adviser–client relationship.

More transparency is welcome but needs to be in a form that is useful to investors and not too burdensome to financial firms.[39] Complete and comparable disclosure around fees that is concise, coupled with disclosures about all potential conflicts of interest, would go a long way toward building trust in advisers and would give investors the information that they need. Survey respondents seemed quite fond of the idea of introducing a clear standard for cost disclosures in the same way as there are standards for performance disclosure.

This issue of enhanced disclosure is being debated at the European level in discussions around the Packaged Retail Investment Products (PRIPs) and the standardization of a key information document (KID) for such products as investment funds, life insurance, retail structured products, and certain types of pension schemes. Other markets have begun to take steps to enhance transparency. For example, in the United States the SEC recently (2009) required enhanced disclosures for mutual funds and required key information to appear in plain English in a standardised order at the front of a mutual fund prospectus.[40]

Information is not useful, however, if those who use it do not know what to do with it. Regulators and financial firms should endeavour to improve investor education so that investors are better informed and better prepared to make the investing decisions that will benefit them over the course of their investing lives. This goal is indeed a long-term project but one with large payoffs for investors and society as a whole.

Financial service providers can better serve clients by offering simplified products to investors with more basic needs and complex products to clients with more specialised needs.

[39]Troy A. Paredes, "Blinded by the Light: Information Overload and Its Consequences for Securities Regulation," *Washington University Law Quarterly* (forthcoming): http://papers.ssrn.com/sol3/papers.cfm?abstract_id=413180.

[40]US SEC, "Enhanced Disclosure and New Prospectus Delivery Option for Registered Open-End Management Investment Companies," Release Nos. 33-8998 (2009): www.sec.gov/rules/final/2009/33-8998.pdf.

One concern we often came across in markets that decided to ban inducements was the fear that such a move would stratify the investing public into the few that could afford investment advice and the many who could not and would thus end up without any advice at all. We encourage regulators and financial advisory firms in all markets to work together to find ways to bring investors greater access to investment advice. The need for investment advice is not all or nothing; it exists along a continuum, with some needing a great deal of advice and some needing none but most investors needing advice somewhere in the middle of that great divide.

The two most popular solutions to mis-selling that did not involve inducement or commission bans were (1) revising commission structures to eliminate those that encourage volume sales (tiered commissions), and (2) setting equal commission levels (as a percentage of management fee) for all products in the same category. We encourage financial advisory firms to explore such reforms as self-regulatory mechanisms that can address some of the conflicts of interest in the adviser–client relationship without the need for outside regulatory forces.

We also encourage financial advisers to invest in consistent and quality adviser training focused on fulfilling the needs of the client so that advisers can better understand their clients' goals and choose better products to help them reach those goals.

Appendix

	Total	Americas	Asia Pacific	EMEA
In your opinion, what are the main causes of mis-selling?				
Inappropriate commission payments by product producers	48%	48%	55%	41%
Inappropriate internal remuneration structures at distributors (skewed toward volume sales or specific products)	70%	68%	75%	71%
Selling pressure from other internal group entities	63%	63%	65%	60%
Lack of professional qualifications	32%	30%	31%	40%
Lack of transparency regarding product comparisons	36%	37%	31%	34%
Laziness	19%	23%	11%	14%
Other	6%	6%	8%	8%
No opinion	2%	3%	1%	1%
Unweighted Sample Size	514	158	91	265

What are the most important reforms needed to combat mis-selling?				
Reforming pay structures at distributors, linking staff and senior management remuneration to good investment outcomes for clients	56%	54%	65%	54%
Completely banning commission payments by product producers	15%	15%	13%	15%
Reforming commission payment structures by product producers (to reduce incentives to favor unsuitable products), while retaining them at least partially	35%	34%	43%	31%
Requiring a minimum standard of professional qualifications	43%	41%	43%	48%
Requiring wider product offerings by all distributors	5%	5%	4%	7%
Improving disclosure of product information to clients	46%	44%	47%	48%
Mandating full disclosure of product cost structures to clients	65%	68%	55%	62%
Mandating clear disclosure of all commission payments received by distributors before investment	60%	64%	55%	51%
Improving redress possibilities for clients (in particular retail clients)	24%	27%	25%	14%

(continued)

	Total	Americas	Asia Pacific	EMEA
Improving enforcement by national regulators	23%	22%	27%	23%
Improving investor education	46%	44%	48%	51%
Other	6%	6%	5%	6%
No opinion	1%	1%	1%	2%
Unweighted Sample Size	514	158	91	265

If commission payments by product producers are banned completely, what consequences, if any, do you see occurring as a result?

	Total	Americas	Asia Pacific	EMEA
Distributors will stop offering particular products altogether, so product choice will diminish.	30%	25%	42%	33%
Retail clients will refuse to pay fees for advice.	16%	10%	21%	32%
Small retail clients will not be able to afford advice.	29%	24%	43%	37%
Distributors will continue to offer advice, but will shrink the product offerings to those they continue to receive fees on.	46%	47%	42%	43%
Distributors will continue to offer advice, but will offer only "in-house" products (products from their own financial group).	38%	38%	32%	45%
Banks will stop offering advice altogether, and will steer client money into deposits.	12%	8%	23%	15%
Small distributors will go out of business, reducing distribution channel choice and reducing product and service choice.	25%	19%	35%	35%
Other	12%	13%	10%	11%
None—I don't see any consequences of a complete ban of commission payments by product producers.	12%	15%	5%	4%
No opinion	6%	6%	4%	7%
Unweighted Sample Size	513	157	91	265

How, if at all, could commission payments by product producers be reformed without a complete ban?

	Total	Americas	Asia Pacific	EMEA
Revising commission structures to eliminate those that encourage volume sales (tiered commissions)	45%	41%	58%	46%
Providing only for minimum remuneration levels to compensate for distribution expenses incurred	17%	18%	15%	14%
Setting equal commission levels (as a fixed percentage of the management fee) for all products in the same category	32%	35%	24%	29%

(continued)

	Total	Americas	Asia Pacific	EMEA
Introducing clear standards for cost disclosures in the same way as there are standards for performance disclosure	68%	68%	62%	73%
Other	7%	8%	8%	4%
No opinion	5%	5%	5%	5%
Unweighted Sample Size	511	157	91	263

How serious do you consider the potential loss of distribution channels and/or the reduction of product range by distributors in case of restrictions or bans on commission payments?

1 - Not serious at all	18%	22%	10%	12%
2	17%	19%	9%	18%
3	21%	22%	21%	18%
4	22%	18%	29%	28%
5 - Very serious	16%	13%	24%	17%
No opinion	6%	6%	8%	7%
Top 2	22%	18%	32%	24%
Unweighted Sample Size	513	157	91	265

Do you have examples of the impact of commission bans implemented through national law?

Yes	8%	6%	11%	10%
No	92%	94%	89%	90%
Unweighted Sample Size	494	153	90	251

Do you have suggested solutions for small retail investors who cannot afford fee-based advice?

Yes	43%	50%	26%	36%
No	57%	50%	74%	64%
Unweighted Sample Size	493	154	89	250

A complete ban on commission payments would be justified, even if it is ultimately damaging for small retail investors.

Agree	21%	22%	16%	22%
Disagree	66%	62%	79%	67%
No opinion	13%	16%	6%	11%
Unweighted Sample Size	506	154	90	262

A complete ban on commission payments would eliminate mis-selling completely.

Agree	10%	8%	18%	10%
Disagree	81%	83%	75%	81%
No opinion	9%	9%	7%	9%
Unweighted Sample Size	507	156	89	262

(continued)

	Total	Americas	Asia Pacific	EMEA
Requiring and enforcing a full disclosure requirement on all commissions and fees paid and to whom would go a long way to solving the issues.				
Agree	83%	86%	79%	73%
Disagree	12%	10%	18%	17%
No opinion	5%	4%	3%	9%
Unweighted Sample Size	505	155	90	260
Greater investor education is required for any regulatory moves associated with mis-selling to be effective.				
Agree	72%	68%	86%	77%
Disagree	17%	20%	11%	13%
No opinion	10%	12%	3%	10%
Unweighted Sample Size	506	155	90	261

CFA Institute

AUTHORS

Claire Fargeot
Head
Standards and Financial Market Integrity
Europe, Middle East, and Africa

Matt Orsagh, CFA, CIPM
Director
Capital Markets Policy

CONTRIBUTORS

Kurt N. Schacht, JD, CFA
Managing Director
Standards and Financial Market Integrity

Robert W. Dannhauser, CFA
Head
Capital Markets Policy

Josina Kamerling
Head
Regulatory Outreach
Europe, Middle East, and Africa

Mirzha de Manuel Aramendia
Director
Capital Markets Policy

Made in the USA
Monee, IL
05 November 2026

67379776R00045